CH00688340

TEAM
LEAD
SUCCEED

NICK FEWINGS

Cover image by: Design Hunters, 99 Designs
Book design by: SWATT Books Ltd

Printed in the United Kingdom
First Printing, 2022

ISBN: 978-1-7397572-0-5 (Paperback)
ISBN: 978-1-7397572-1-2 (eBook)

Nick Fewings
Bournemouth, Dorset

www.ngagementworks.com

DEDICATION

This book is dedicated to Zippo, our much loved and much missed Greek rescue dog, whose joy of his daily walks helped spark many creative ideas included in this book, apart from when I had to concentrate on picking up his poop.

CONTENTS

Dedication   3

CHAPTER 1:   Background and Structure   7
CHAPTER 2:   Who Is in Your Team?   23
CHAPTER 3:   How Effective Is Your Teamwork?   57
CHAPTER 4:   The Team DyNAmics Model   61
CHAPTER 5:   Purpose: Element 1 of 16   73
CHAPTER 6:   Trust: Element 2 of 16   81
CHAPTER 7:   Planning: Element 3 of 16   91
CHAPTER 8:   Collaboration: Element 4 of 16   107
CHAPTER 9:   Accountability: Element 5 of 16   117
CHAPTER 10:   Commitment: Element 6 of 16   125
CHAPTER 11:   Roles & Skills: Element 7 of 16   135
CHAPTER 12:   Communication: Element 8 of 16   143
CHAPTER 13:   Decision-Making: Element 9 of 16   155
CHAPTER 14:   Team Meetings: Element 10 of 16   163
CHAPTER 15:   Processes: Element 11 of 16   171
CHAPTER 16:   Environment: Element 12 of 16   183
CHAPTER 17:   Vision: Element 13 of 16   191
CHAPTER 18:   Diversity: Element 14 of 16   199
CHAPTER 19:   Reflection: Element 15 of 16   211
CHAPTER 20:   Transformation: Element 16 of 16   221
CHAPTER 21:   Exploring Leadership   231

Get in Touch   253

Acknowledgements   255

About the Author   257

Endnotes   259

CHAPTER 1:

BACKGROUND AND STRUCTURE

If you work as part of a team, I have written this book for you.

We spend a large proportion of our careers working in teams. On average, in the UK, we work between 45 to 50 years of our life, and spend 35% of our waking hours during this period working, a lot of which will be as part of a team.

It is therefore important that this time is both fulfilling and positive, not only for you but for your colleagues as well.

Let me be brutally honest, if the team that you are a part of is not working effectively, it can feel awful and often has a knock-on effect on how you feel outside of work, and I am sure that some of you reading this will have experienced this, as I have.

Over the years that I have been facilitating high-performance teamwork and speaking at conferences about this topic, individuals will regularly come up to me and either say that they do not like the job they do, how their team is working, or indeed how they are being led.

I always say to them that it is no good just moaning about this to others outside of your team; for things to change, you need to take action and speak up, as everyone in a team has a voice.

My goal, in writing this book, is to share with you my knowledge and experience about teamwork, so that if you read something and realise that it causes you or your team a problem, you can do something about it, by speaking up and sharing your thoughts with your colleagues.

It is also an opportunity for you to celebrate what is working well, and if needs be just make some tweaks to "squeeze some more juice from the orange", so that you can become even more effective.

Now before you get into the detail of this book, I think it is only fair and right of me to let you know what it is and what it is not.

It is not a how-to manual about creating the perfect high-performing team, as I believe that this is almost unachievable. There are so many different factors that affect teamwork that you will never get them all exactly right at the same time.

Firstly, you and your colleagues in your team will all be different, both behaviourally and also with regards to the technical skills and experience that you bring. In addition, your team is likely to constantly change, with colleagues leaving and others joining.

Secondly, the environment in which your team works will be different to other teams. Even within an organisation, the objectives of your team, your goals, strengths and challenges, will be different to a team that may only work a few feet away from yours, albeit you will have some organisational cultural similarities.

Thirdly, because we are all behaviourally and technically unique, those who lead teams will have their own unique style, which will impact on the team.

And lastly, the environment in which your team works will be affected by different factors, both internally and externally, and therefore will constantly change.

So, due to these many factors that influence teamwork, perfection is, I believe, unachievable. However what I can guarantee is that seeking perfection will lead you and your team to achieving truly remarkable things and even greater success.

What I hope this book is, however, is a valuable resource, with real-life stories and practical learning about teamwork and leading teams, to enhance your teamwork and team effectiveness.

Now I have never been one to say to both individuals and teams that if you do something, you will definitely get this result, as I do not know well enough the people in your team, nor the environment that your team works in.

So, what this book aims to achieve is to get you thinking about practical ideas that would work for you and your team, that you may consider applying to your specific team's circumstances.

For those of you who were born in the UK, or who have lived in the UK for a while, you will know that the British have a wonderful ability to understate our satisfaction and pleasure.

So I hope that after applying some or indeed all of the learning in this book with your team, when someone asks you, "How's work been this week?", that it elevates your reply from "Not too bad" to "It's been OK", or indeed the euphoric response of "Quite good actually".

Unless I have been part of your team, led a team you've been part of, facilitated team development with you over the last 20 years, or you have been in the audience of one of the hundreds of conferences that I have spoken at, we have probably not met in person, so I think it is only fair and proper before you go any further that I share with you how this book has come to be, what the title means and a bit about myself, so you know me a little bit better.

LOCKDOWN BRINGS OPPORTUNITY

"That was brilliant; I learnt so much about myself, my colleagues and how to enhance our teamwork. Have you written a book, so I can read more?" This is a question I have been asked many times over the years.

My reply has always been no, up until the 23rd March 2020, the date of the first UK lockdown due to the COVID-19 pandemic.

During the first week of March, my wife and I had gone on vacation to Dubai, for some guaranteed sunshine and relaxation at the end of the British winter. This time, however, the atmosphere was different, as the pandemic started to impact tourism.

There were far less travellers and a subdued atmosphere pervaded the hotel, poolside, restaurants and beaches. It was as though people had a subconscious understanding of the enormity of what was to come and the impact it would have on everyone's life.

The week after our return from Dubai, I travelled to York to facilitate a team development workshop, which unbeknown to me at the time would be the last I would undertake face to face for 15 months.

Twelve days later, we were in lockdown and my diary, which had been filled with both team development facilitation and conference speaking, suddenly was free, as bookings were cancelled.

As in previous times of economic hardship and uncertainty, one of the first things to be cancelled by companies is learning and development, with budgets and cashflow being diverted to essential operations to keep businesses afloat and staff in work.

The majority of my work is in the UK, however bookings to work with teams in various European countries also disappeared, as did my planned conference talks in Europe, the USA, the Far East and the Middle East.

From a full diary of bookings to zero took about three weeks.

Now, I have always been an optimist. Over my 59 years, I have experienced what are reported to be life's most stressful challenges, and have come out the other side, so I did as I always have done: looked at my situation from a positive perspective and thought about the opportunities that may present themselves.

My first thought was to help as many people as I knew that might be struggling from a wellbeing perspective, due to the massive impact that the pandemic was having on them.

I wrote and published articles about the behaviours that people were exhibiting and how not to be surprised at some of the unusual behaviours that people might experience themselves and also observe in others. The key was helping people to understand that these unusual behaviours were normal in times of massive change, especially when the change was predominantly outside of their control.

In addition, I provided people with hints and tips about what they could do to enable themselves to focus on the things that they could control and reduce the amount of stress that they were experiencing.

Now, to help me reach as wide an audience as I could with my articles of support, I enrolled on an online course on how to maximise LinkedIn. Bizarrely, the excellent course I came across was run by someone with the same surname as me, however no relation, namely Alice Fewings. Her course helped me to reach more of my LinkedIn connections and followers.

On the same course was Karen Williams, The Book Mentor. Karen and I struck up a conversation and this provided me with the idea to write this book.

I realised that the pandemic had provided me with an opportunity to dedicate quality time to writing, as I had gained time from not having to travel to facilitate team development and speak at conferences.

So even though, over the time since the pandemic started, I have pivoted to delivering team development and conference speaking online, it also provided me with the opportunity of time, which I had previously spent travelling, to focus on writing.

Enrolling on Karen's Smart Author System course and following the invaluable hints and tips included, combined with the time that I had available, has resulted in this book.

WHY TEAM LEAD SUCCEED?

Apart from projects and business start-ups, more often than not, in business, a team already exists. Leaders are either appointed or chosen from within the team or recruited from another part of the business or externally. They may reshuffle the team that they join, however the team exists.

A leader is therefore another member of the team, albeit that they have ultimate accountability and responsibility for their team members and their team's performance.

This book is therefore structured to focus on teamwork, with one chapter near the end of the book dedicated to leadership.

So whether you are a team member or a leader, this book includes learning, hints and tips that will help you.

As a team member, you should have a vested interest in how your team is performing, as it is likely that this will impact on your financial remuneration and personal wellbeing. In addition, at some point you are likely to secure a leadership role, so the learning about leadership in this book will hopefully stand you in good stead for the future.

If you are already a leader, it is good to know that you are reading this book, as that can only mean one thing, that you are interested in continuing to learn and develop as a leader.

So, whoever you are or whatever your role is in work, I am glad that you are here, as it only means one thing: you want to learn and are motivated to make your teamwork even better than it is currently.

There are a number of variations of a quote that essentially says that the day we stop learning should be the day that we die, and I believe this is true. I would implore you to learn from others at every opportunity.

This book is therefore written with three types of reader in mind.

Firstly, team members. Your opinion is important, to ensure that you and your colleagues are working in a positive team environment that enables individuals to be appreciated for the knowledge and skills that they bring and the part that they play in achieving team goals. If things are not working as well as expected, things will only change if they are highlighted and discussed with the rest of the team.

Secondly, this book is dedicated to all those leaders who have been appointed into a leadership position, quite often with little or no prior training or support. I hope it helps you to avoid going through the pain I did by having to learn from my mistakes in my first leadership role.

Finally, it is dedicated to those leaders who wish to continue to develop and grow. Hopefully you will read something new that you can use, to enhance your leadership skills or the effectiveness of how you lead your team or your teamwork.

STRUCTURE OF THE BOOK

I have structured this book similar to a recipe book, in that there are core ingredients that support high-performance teamwork, which every team should focus on. Then there are the additional ingredients that will enhance your teamwork.

Now depending on how good you and your team are already in particular aspects of your teamwork, you may need a sprinkling of some of the learning in particular chapters. There may be other areas of teamwork where you need a couple of heaped tablespoons, to really enhance what you are doing.

The beauty of this book is that, based on your knowledge and experience of your team and how effective your teamwork is in particular areas, it will enable you to pick and choose the ingredients you need and how much of each you require.

> *"There is nothing more satisfying than being part of*
> *a team, or indeed leading a team, that achieves a*
> *goal that was originally thought unachievable."*

WHAT EXACTLY IS A TEAMOLOGIST?

Teamologist is a word that I use to describe what I have done for the last 30 years and continue to do.

My definition of a teamologist is a person who studies the dynamics of teamwork, and uses this knowledge and experience to help teams become more effective and achieve greater success.

I have always been fascinated by teamwork. This fascination started when I was part of a team, continued when I led teams and finally, it was something that I was able to dedicate my full attention to when, 20 years ago, I began to facilitate team development and speak about teamwork at conferences around the world, and in doing so, was recognised by others as a specialist.

My fascination with teamwork started at the outset of my career, as a 19-year-old fresh from school with mediocre exam results. I joined Barclays Bank and my first job was in my city of birth, Plymouth, in the South West of the UK.

Resplendent in my dark blue pinstriped three-piece suit, I arrived on my first day, to be buddied with another member of the branch who took me through my induction, part of which was to meet the team that my first job would be in.

Various promotions ensued, together with moves to new teams and different branches throughout the South West region. After ten years, I began working at the regional office, still as part of a team and at the top of the clerical grades.

During these first ten years, I experienced the good, the bad and the ugly of teamwork. I knew how it felt to be working in a team that was successful and achieving our targets and goals, and how positive the working environment was and, indeed, the positive impact this had on my life outside of work.

I also experienced working in a team that was struggling and that awful feeling on a Sunday evening, knowing that I had to go to work again on Monday morning, for another week as part of a dysfunctional team. I also knew what it was like to work in a toxic team, with fractured relationships and individuals out for their own success.

Fortunately, my experiences of working in good teams far outweighed the negative times, but all the teams I was part of gave me invaluable learning experiences.

Then, 30 years ago, I became a leader of a team for the first time. Up until this time, I had been known for my technical expertise and worked as part of a team. Leading a team was the next step on my career ladder.

My elation soon turned to misery, as I quickly became aware that being a technical expert does not necessarily make you a great leader. Whilst I had lots of experience of working as part of a team, I had no experience of leading one.

Since those early days of leading a team for the first time, and things going badly wrong, I have continually listened and learned, to enhance my leadership skills and importantly apply them to create a positive and successful working environment for my teams, so that both individuals and the team achieved the personal and collective success that they deserved.

FROM STATEMENTS TO STAGES

So how did my journey to becoming a teamologist happen?

Well, as briefly mentioned already, as an inexperienced 19-year-old, with mediocre exam results, I decided to get a job with Barclays Bank. Why? Well, quite simply and naively, I thought that it would be like playing Monopoly with real money! How wrong I was.

My first job in Barclays, in 1981, was putting customers' bank statements into envelopes and posting them out to them. This was long before the time of internet banking, so everything was done manually. I used to hate the end and beginning of each month, when I would go to work and be faced with a huge pile of statements. Each statement had to be ripped along the perforation, folded and placed into an envelope.

What made it worse was that some statements did not have the customer's address on them, so I had to find that from their records and write it onto their statement. Secondly, some customers insisted on having their cheques returned with their statement, which required going to each customer's document drawer, retrieving their cheques, and then ticking off each one against those shown on their statement.

Overall, however, I thoroughly enjoyed the different jobs that I undertook over the next 20 years, including cashier, loans officer, securities clerk, an operational manager (my first opportunity to lead others), then a project manager, which ultimately ended up with me becoming a change leader, helping to communicate new strategy and direction and what it meant for staff affected by these changes. During this time, I led many different teams, in various locations in the UK including some which had staff overseas.

However, never in my wildest dreams would I have guessed, after 20 years working for Barclays, that in my second career I would become a highly-regarded global facilitator of team development and be deemed a specialist in helping teams to achieve high performance, working with many well-known global brands. Not only this but that I would also become an award-winning conference speaker, delivering keynote speeches about teamwork at conferences in Europe, the Middle East, the Far East and the USA, clocking up many hundreds of conferences to date in front of audiences of all sizes, including some of over 600 delegates.

My passion, in understanding how to achieve high-performance teamwork, has also led me to create the Team DyNAmics Model, which helps teams measure their effectiveness across 16 areas of teamwork, or as I call them, Elements. The model is used by teams around the globe and there are 16 chapters in this book dedicated to each of the Elements in the model.

So, how did I get from banking to being recognised as a teamologist?

Well, they say that there is opportunity waiting for us around every corner and mine was waiting for me in the shape of a great guy called Mike Jones, an inspirational and highly-regarded fellow facilitator and speaker, who also used to work for Barclays.

I was leading the cultural change of two departments becoming one. I needed to create a shared culture that would support the new way of working and get the people from both departments to embrace their new unity. A colleague said that they knew a man who could help, who was Mike. He opened my eyes to the power of behavioural psychology in a colourful way, and demonstrated how it was an effective foundation upon which to enhance both individual relationships and teamwork.

After a spell working on a global project in London, due to redundancies I had the opportunity to spread my wings and leave Barclays, utilising the excellent training and experience I had received to set up my first training company and share my knowledge with other organisations and teams, helping them achieve greater success.

The rest, all 20 years of it, is history and my hope is that this book becomes part of my legacy.

HEAVY ON PRACTICAL LEARNING, LIGHT ON THEORY

Over the years, I have read many books about teamwork and leadership, and indeed, undertaken many courses relating to these subjects, coming across many models and theories.

The learning, books, models and theories that I have always remembered are those which have been practical. By this I mean that when there has been a theory or model explained, the ones that have been invaluable to me, and that I have used, have been those that I have been able to apply practically and which have achieved positive results.

So, whilst there are theories and models included in this book, they are all ones that I have been able to apply practically and know they work, and so they should therefore be of value to you too.

STORYTELLING

No doubt, like me, you like a good story. From an early age, our parents would tell us stories, many of which would have a lesson. It is ingrained in our psyche to learn from storytelling, which has happened since the human race was able to communicate verbally. Even prior to verbal communication, storytelling occurred, as can be witnessed by the cave paintings of our ancestors.

Bearing this in mind, I have included stories throughout this book. Some have been altered slightly to uphold anonymity of individuals and teams, however the core of every story is true and each has a lesson that is applicable to the learning in the particular chapter or section of the book in which it is included.

QUOTATIONS

I do not think I am alone in thoroughly enjoying a good quotation and I have used them throughout my working career to open up conversations with others, getting them to share their thoughts, perspectives and ideas.

I have therefore used quotations throughout this book and unless I name someone as the person that the quotation is attributed to, it will be mine. I hope that you enjoy them and that they get you thinking about your team and your teamwork.

Some quotations will have an image as a background. As a keen amateur photographer, these images have been taken by myself, unless I have acknowledged the photographer.

LEARNING WITH LAUGHTER

Over the years that I have facilitated or spoken at a conference, there have been many funny moments. I have shared some of these, which include a relevant lesson. They include some that I am regularly asked to include as part of my facilitation or conference speaking, namely The Greatest Lover and The Doctor's Surgery. I hope that they put a smile on your face.

THE POWER OF 4

As you read this book, you will see that the number 4, or multiples of 4, occur regularly. Why? Quite simply, it is recognised that our brains cope well with 4 and multiples of it, which help us to remember what we have read.

THE TWO MAIN INGREDIENTS: THE WHO AND THE HOW

Achieving high-performance teamwork is similar to creating a meal. There are certain ingredients in a meal that are essential. For instance, in a cookery book that I was reading recently, the author wrote that every Indian dish is based on a trinity of spices and that turmeric powder and chilli powder are the mother and father of curries and at the heart of the trinity of spices.

It is similar with high-performance teamwork: the two main ingredients are knowing **WHO** is in your team and **HOW** effective your teamwork is.

Knowing **WHO** is in your team enables you to play to people's strengths and, if within your job remit, to lead, coach, motivate and inspire individuals in a way that meets their needs, so that they feel valued for their contribution in achieving team goals, and additionally can develop as individuals.

If you think about the majority of teams in sport that achieve success, the managers or coaches of those teams spend a huge amount of time ensuring that the right person, with the right skills, plays in the most appropriate position to maximise the use of those skills and that the rest of the team also know what the unique skills of their colleagues are.

Time is also invested in understanding the individuals in the team, from a behavioural perspective. How do they make decisions? What are their communication needs and their communication styles? What motivates them? What challenges them? What happens when they are under stress?

All the above are also totally applicable to a business team and therefore you need to know not only what you bring to your team, but importantly what others in your team bring, enabling you to understand the strengths and possible challenges of your team.

Knowing **HOW** effective your teamwork is has a direct impact on the Key Performance Indicators (KPIs) that your team has been set. These indicators are likely to be measures such as actual spend versus budget, quality of output, or of key deadlines or timescales achieved.

Your team's performance against these KPIs is a product of the collective efforts of the people in your team. So, you may think that your team is doing very well because your KPIs are telling you so, however, if you do not know how effective your teamwork is, how do you know whether in fact you could be doing better?

Say, for instance, that your team is achieving 75% of your KPIs, so doing reasonably well. What if you measured your team effectiveness and found out that this was 65%? Just think about the positive impact it would have on your KPIs if you got your team effectiveness up to 80%!

The Team DyNAmics Model that I created, and which is used by teams to measure their team effectiveness as a whole and across 16 Elements of teamwork, provides the **HOW**.

Essentially, these are the other ingredients of teamwork, with some having a greater impact on teamwork than others, and therefore requiring more attention to make sure that they are working effectively. Each of these 16 Elements has a chapter of its own in this book and is explored in more depth.

So the primary focus of this book is to explore in more detail both the **WHO** and the **HOW** of achieving high-performance teamwork, to help and support you in your role within your team and also help your colleagues.

Whilst it is not essential that you read through the chapters in sequence, my suggestion is that in the first instance you do. Subsequently, you can dive into the chapters that are important for you to read at a particular moment in time.

So let us begin with WHO is in your team.

CHAPTER 2:

WHO IS IN YOUR TEAM?

So, who is in your team? Is this a question that you have asked yourself? You might be thinking, of course I know who is in my team, and going through the names of your colleagues in your head. However, knowing who is in your team goes much deeper than just knowing their names.

When I talk about knowing **WHO** is in your team, there are two generic skills that each and every one of us brings to a team. We bring our technical skills, and we also bring our behavioural skills.

So let us explore both in more detail.

TECHNICAL SKILLS

Technical skills are things that we have learnt, to help us do our day-to-day job as effectively as possible, and everyone in your team will have many different ones, including you.

It may be a degree that you obtained at university, self-study at night school or online, or a course that a company you have worked for organised.

Whether it is a degree in accountancy, certification in project management, or accreditation on a course for using PowerPoint effectively, invariably some or all of these technical skills will be of value to both you and your colleagues in your team, to help you achieve your team goals.

So it is important that your colleagues are aware of your technical skills and vice versa, so that you and your team can play to each other's strengths and use each other's expertise to help you as a team achieve your goals.

You would be surprised at how many teams do not know each other's technical skills. Be honest, do you know the technical skills of all your colleagues in your team, and do they know yours?

I never knew you had those skills!

"If we do not know the technical skills and
abilities of our colleagues, how can we utilise
them for the benefit of our team?"

I was working with a team and during one of the discussions, a team member mentioned a legal issue that they had recently spent a lot of time getting to the bottom of, relating to a contract with a supplier.

One of the other team members asked why they had not spoken to them, as they had a legal degree with a focus on contract law. Quite simply, the other team member said that they had not spoken to them because they were unaware of the technical skills that the other person had. Not only had the team member spent a lot of time sorting out the issue, but they had also had to pay a legal firm to provide their expertise and advice. If only they had known!

The suggestion

An effective way to ensure that everyone in your team knows the skills of other team members is to create a Skills Matrix: a simple document that includes each team member's name and then a list of the technical skills that they bring to the team.

Now, the important thing to remember is that you do not want a long list with a lot of irrelevant skills included on it, but you do not want to miss anything either.

So, initially, get each team member to list **ALL** their technical skills. Then at the next opportunity when all your team are together, allow each person to share the skills that they have written down.

Then get the rest of the team to challenge any that they think are not relevant, based on the purpose and goals of your team.

By doing the above, you will then have a list that all the team have bought into and agreed.

Finally, ensure that the list is kept somewhere where all the team have access to it and that it is also updated whenever a new member joins the team or a team member leaves.

If there is a degree of stability in your team, with no changes in team members, you may want to diarise to review your Skills Matrix, say once a quarter, to capture any changes in technical skills that team members may have acquired during the interim period.

The benefits of the team sharing their technical skills include:

1. Knowing who the subject matter experts are in particular technical skills.
2. It reduces the need to seek support outside of the team, whether this be with other parts of the business or someone external to the organisation, when you may need to pay for those services.

3. It can help raise awareness of particular technical skills and help with the development of individuals. For instance, someone in the team who is an expert in PowerPoint might be given a time slot at a team meeting, to provide tips to other members of the team.

4. More in-depth, one-to-one knowledge sharing can help reduce risks when a member of the team is away from work and someone needs to complete some of their tasks, which require them to use some of the technical skills that they have.

I hope that you can now appreciate the benefits of everyone in your team knowing the technical skills of others in the team.

BEHAVIOURAL SKILLS

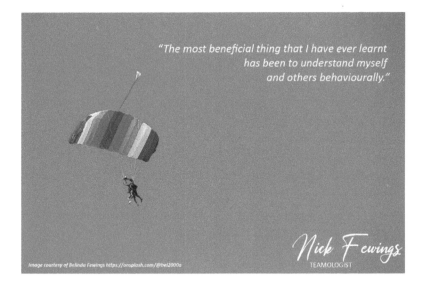

"The most beneficial thing that I have ever learnt has been to understand myself and others behaviourally."

Image courtesy of Belinda Fewings https://onsplash.com/@bel2000a

Nick Fewings
TEAMOLOGIST

What you are about to read about our behaviours is based on the psychology of Carl Jung, a Swiss psychologist, known as the father of modern-day psychology. Jung was born in 1875 and died in 1961 and his studies have been used and continue to be used around the world to this day.

Now the purists, or indeed psychologists, who may read this book may think that by applying his work to four primary colours I am trivialising the great man's work. Far from it.

Applying colours to his work is both effective and practical, to better understand yourself and those who you work with. I have been using colours to bring to life Jung's work for over 30 years, and the impact on individuals and teams has been overwhelmingly positive, based on the feedback from clients.

After all, you do not need to fully understand how a car engine works to be a competent driver and drive your passengers safely and efficiently to your destination. It is the same with overlaying four colours to the work of Jung.

It provides a shorthand for individuals and teams to discuss behavioural preferences in a positive way and importantly have conversations about behaviours that they may never have had previously.

> *"All the world is queer save thee and me,*
> *and even thou art a little queer."*

I think that this saying, attributed to Robert Owen who was born in 1771, sums up behavioural differences quite nicely.

Let us be honest, we do struggle at times with people who do not behave, communicate and think like we do. It just one of those facts of life.

Exit surveys consistently state that of those people who leave a company, at least 50% say they do so *"because of a poor relationship with their boss"*.[1] This figure does not include those who have left because of a personality clash with a colleague either. Maybe you have left a company for this very reason or know someone who has?

I am sure you will agree that the above is a shocking statistic, so understanding behavioural preferences can only be a positive thing for you and your team.

My hope is that reading this chapter will help you have two paradigm shifts with regards to other people. Rather than seeing them as difficult, you will see them just as different to you, and rather than being frustrated by how they do things, you will be fascinated that they do things differently and often achieve as good, or even better outcomes than you do.

How do you like yours?

I first experienced people's preferences in business in my first full-time job, as the office junior with Barclays Bank. Naively, I thought that I would immediately be a cashier, helping customers to pay in or withdraw their money. How wrong I was!

I was to shadow the incumbent office junior, who had been in situ for six months, to take over their duties as they had been promoted into another role.

At 10 am on my second morning, as my first day had been a day of induction, the current office junior took great delight in letting me know that it was time to undertake the tea and coffee run for the 40+ staff of the branch.

This was long before vending machines, so I was taken to the communal kitchen, to be presented with the huge metal water urn, on the top shelf of a wheeled trolley. Beside it was a large teapot, refined and unrefined sugar, loose tea, tea bags and coffee.

On the lower two shelves was a selection of mugs, cups, saucers and spoons. A selection of biscuits were then taken from a cupboard.

The office junior who I was to succeed then produced a tattered and stained notebook. They turned to the first page and explained that this was the page for the management, as they had their drinks served first.

Beside each name was a series of columns. Each column was headed up with a different preference, whether they had tea or coffee, whether they had milk or not, how strong they liked their drink, whether they had sugar and which type and how many spoonfuls. Did they have biscuits and if so, which.

Under each name were two rows, AM and PM, as some had a different preference depending on whether it was the morning or afternoon.

The names of those staff who had moved on had been struck through with pen.

My mentor advised me that this was probably the most important job I would undertake each day, as getting it right had an impact on the mood of the staff.

After a nervous start, I soon began to enjoy the twice-daily refreshment run and took great joy, by the end of my sixth month as the office junior, in having memorised the preferences of all the staff in the branch.

This was the first time that I had really thought about the preferences that we all have, and if you think about it, we have many. The different foods we enjoy, comedy and comedians that make us laugh, our favourite bands and music, the sports we like, the cars we drive, the vacations that we enjoy and lots more that I am sure you can think of.

In terms of teamwork, an understanding of our behavioural preferences is of huge importance. Let me explain.

As human beings, we all tend to be curious about what makes us the person we are, or "what makes us tick". Why we think the way we do, why we make decisions and communicate in a particular way, why we use some behaviours regularly and struggle with others.

And our curiosity does not stop there either, as we then turn our attention to how others behave, especially those who behave differently to us.

Over the years, I have heard people say things such as:

"If they did it my way, it would be so much easier."

"Don't they realise that the answer is staring them in the face?"

"Why can't they be more like me?"

"No matter how many times I explain it, they just aren't getting it!"

All the above are examples of people not understanding behavioural differences and getting frustrated with people that are behaviourally different to themselves.

Understanding behavioural preferences, both yours and those of others, enables you to do a number of things.

1. Play to your strengths
Each of us brings some wonderful behavioural strengths to a team. Some are good at making decisive decisions, focussed on achieving goals, whilst others are good at considering things from another person's perspective. Some have an incredible eye for detail, so that mistakes are not made, whilst others are great at seeing the big picture, what is happening beyond the day-to-day working of the team.

Don't get me wrong, we all have challenges, however my belief is that we should only try to overcome or master those areas of challenge if we know that they potentially hold us back in our role, or we are aware that they upset other people on a regular basis.

It is far better to continue to develop your strengths, but to be mindful of your challenges and only focus on overcoming those that you know impact you and others negatively.

2. Appreciate that there are many ways to achieve success
The teams that I have worked with who have achieved greater success in teamwork are invariably made up of heterogeneous members,

heterogeneous meaning diverse in character. Individuals are appreciated and valued for being different, both behaviourally and also for bringing different technical skills to the team.

Homogeneous teams are often the ones that struggle, homogeneous meaning alike or similar. Behaviourally, they are likely to think, make decisions and communicate in a very similar way and additionally have similar technical skillsets.

Whilst there may be a high degree of harmony within homogeneous teams, because individuals are likely to agree with each other, the team is likely to struggle to transform and do things better, as they will have a fixed mindset about how to go about things. Creativity and exploration of different ways to do things may be a struggle for teams like this.

Creating a team which has both different technical skills and behavioural skills is more likely to give you a greater opportunity for success, as the different behavioural preferences will enable the sharing and discussion of different ideas to shape the future, or indeed different suggested solutions to overcome challenges that the team face. Whatever the team decide is the best thing to do, then the different technical skills of the team can come into play.

3. Communicate in a way that people with different communication needs buy into

Each of us has our own communication style, but we must not forget that others will have different communication needs to ours. A degree of flexibility, to get your message landing with as many people as possible, is really important.

The most effective communication is that which is delivered and includes information that resonates with the broadest audience possible, based on their communication needs.

As an example, if you are communicating a message about the introduction of a new piece of technology that your team will be expected to use, you might construct your message to ensure that it includes the benefits of the new technology, what features it will have that make it interesting to use, how individuals will be supported to learn to use it and how to understand the technical details of using it and any risks involved.

4. Collaborate with team members, in a way that recognises their learning style and motivations

The well-known phrase "Different strokes for different folks" is so relevant. Some may learn by being set challenging goals to achieve, others by the opportunity to learn from a 1:1 coaching style. Some learn by reading and absorbing knowledge and information, whilst others learn by the opportunity to test out the learning in a safe environment, enabling them to learn from their success and also their failures.

In terms of our behaviours, there is often no right or wrong way, there is just difference. By valuing and appreciating these differences, we can reduce stress and frustration and increase the opportunities that behavioural diversity in a team presents us with.

Now before we delve deeper into behavioural preferences, I thought it would be useful to take a trip back in time and explore the history of these differences.

IT ALL BEGAN WITH HIPPOCRATES

The study of human behaviour is nothing new and goes back over 2,500 years. One of those, if not the first, to be recognised for studying human behaviour was Hippocrates.

Hippocrates was a Greek physician and is often described as "the Father of Medicine". The most widely recognised reason that people have heard of him today is due to the Hippocratic oath.

The oath, accredited to Hippocrates (although some contest whether it was him who wrote it), is still, albeit in a slightly altered form, used in the medical world today. It includes medical ethics, such as medical confidentiality and non-maleficence. In fact, a lot of countries still require their medical students to swear by the oath, as a rite of passage, before they practise medicine.

Hippocrates was born in 460 BCE and lived on the Greek island of Kos (or Cos) and if you are fortunate to visit it and go to Kos town centre, you will see a plane or plantane tree, that is surrounded by railings and shored up by metal posts. It is purported that the original tree, from which the current one has grown, was where Hippocrates undertook his studies with his pupils, all those years ago.

Up until the time that Hippocrates came along, it was felt that the way in which people behaved was influenced by the gods who, when we were born, looked upon us and decided what type of person and behaviours we were going to have and also what diseases we would get.

Hippocrates disagreed with this. He had studied people that had come to him for his medical skills and knowledge, who had similar ailments and who he realised behaved in different ways. He termed these different behaviours "temperaments" and identified four of them.

These four types of behaviours were associated with "humours", different bodily fluids that determined the way in which someone behaved, humour being derived from the Latin for moisture.

The choleric, with an excess of yellow bile, was seen as a quick thinker and driven.

The sanguine, with an excess of blood, was seen as optimistic and outgoing.

The phlegmatic, with an excess of phlegm, was seen as relaxed and peaceful.

The melancholic, with an excess of black bile, was seen as analytical and quiet.

Medical practitioners believed the work of Hippocrates and said that if you behaved normally, you were at ease with yourself. However, if you behaved with a high degree of one of the four extremes, they said you had a dis-ease, hence the word disease that we use today.

If you exhibited one of the extremes, they would undertake a medical procedure to alleviate your symptoms: bloodletting for the sanguines, and a mild poison for the cholerics to get them to retch up their yellow bile. For the phlegmatics, a cough medicine to get rid of their excess phlegm and finally, for the melancholics, trepanning (drilling a hole through your head), as they thought the black bile, which does not actually exist, made your brain swell!

Medical practices such as the above continued well into the 19th century.

As an example and to bring these four temperaments to life, let me share with you a typical conversation that each of these four types may have had with Hippocrates, each having the same ailment of a sore arm.

The choleric, with an excess of yellow bile: "Good morning Hippocrates, I have come to see you as I know you are the best doctor in the area. I have a problem with my arm that I need you to examine; tell me what is wrong and advise me what I need to do to put it right. I need you to do this within five minutes, as I am extremely busy."

The sanguine, with an excess of blood: "Hi doctor, how are you doing? I have come to see you as I have a problem with my arm and I've heard that you are amazing. It happened recently when I had friends around. We were having a laugh and a joke, and I decided to do a cartwheel, to make them laugh. Well, I have never been much good at gymnastics and I fell on my arm and hurt it. I am hoping you can sort it out, as I have some more friends coming around in the next week, and if you can sort it out, I would love to invite you to join us."

The phlegmatic, with an excess of phlegm: "Sorry to trouble you, doctor, as I know that you are very busy. I have a bit of a sore arm. It started when I was out walking my dog. We got to a river and had to cross it.

Now my dog does not like water, so I had to pick it up in my arms. I did not realise how much weight it had put on recently and as I lifted it, I felt a twinge in my arm. It has carried on for a few days and hence I decided I needed to see you. Now, whilst I was waiting to see you, I noticed that there were a lot of other people waiting to see you as well. I also noticed that they looked a lot worse than me, so I felt that as I only have a slight ache in my arm, that you should pay attention to their wellbeing and if it is OK with you, I will come back on another day, when hopefully you will be a little quieter. Is that all right with you?"

The melancholic, with an excess of black bile: "Good afternoon doctor. I have come to see you, as I have an issue with my arm that I need you to rectify. It started when I was in my garden, turning the compacted earth with my spade. I was exerting significant pressure on the blade with my left foot when I experienced a sharp shooting pain. This excruciating pain went into my tibia, then into my fibula, across my patella and into my femur. It then travelled across my pelvic girdle, moved vertically up my spinal column, into my clavicle, then into my humerus, and finally, into my ulna and radius.

"I know this, because I immediately went into my house, into my library, and checked my medical dictionary. I believe that I know what is wrong with my arm, however wish to hear what you have to say about it, before I go to appointments with another two doctors, to hear what they have to say."

I hope that the above has provided you with a pen portrait of the four temperaments and the behaviours associated with them and that you may already have associated with the style of one of them yourself, or indeed recognised it in other people that you know!

Fortunately, as previously mentioned, the Swiss psychologist Carl Gustav Jung undertook his own studies of human behaviour and argued that we are all different based on what he called psychological attitudes and functions. Jung's work still continues to be valid and used today, and has resulted in various behavioural profiling tools and techniques being developed.

JUNGIAN PSYCHOLOGY

Now whilst I have used Jungian psychology to help both teams and leaders to value and appreciate behavioural differences, what I share with you in this book is not an in-depth explanation of Jung's psychology, but rather a shorthand, practical version, which should be sufficient for you to begin to understand yourself and your team better.

If you are intrigued by what you read and want to study the work of Carl Jung in greater depth, please do so.

Attitudes and functions

Jung said that we are all unique, due to the extent to which we use 3 pairs of psychological preferences. He documented 2 attitudes and 4 functions, that make each of us unique, due to the degree and combinations in which we use them.

We can use all of them

Now I cannot emphasise enough that these psychological attitudes and functions that we use are preferences and that we are able to access all of them. Sometimes if we have a strong preference for one over another, we may find it more difficult to access and use the other, but we can do it, and like anything in life, if we practise using it, over time we will find it easier to use.

Let me provide you with an analogy to better explain what I mean.

Each of us has a preferred writing hand, the one that feels more comfortable to use.

If you injured your preferred writing hand, you would still be able to write with your other hand, albeit it would not feel as comfortable, nor likely as legible as writing with your preferred writing hand, until you had continued to use it for a long period of time.

It is the same with the psychological preferences that I will explain shortly. They are preferences and we can use all of them.

Another analogy that demonstrates preferences is folding our arms. We all fold our arms in a way that feels comfortable to us, which is our preferred way of doing it. If I asked you to fold your arms in your preferred way and then asked you to fold your arms the other way, you would invariably find it awkward to do at first and it would feel uncomfortable. However, if you continued to unfold your arms and fold them in your less preferred way, over time it would not feel so bad and indeed, you would be able to do it quicker.

If you don't believe me, put this book down and give it a try. Firstly, fold your arms your preferred way and then unfold them and fold them in the opposite way to your normal preference. I would imagine that it feels awkward to you. Now unfold them and fold them again in the opposite way to your normal preference. Do this maybe half a dozen times and by the end of it, you are likely to find it easier to do and less awkward.

You can undertake the above activity with your colleagues. It is great fun to watch everyone doing this and also observing the different preferences of your colleagues. Some will have their fingers showing over their biceps, others keep their fingers hidden, some fold left arm over right and others, right arm over left.

As we all know, there is no right or wrong way to fold our arms and therefore it is a great way of demonstrating the preferences that we have and a good way to open up discussion about the 2 attitudes and 4 functions that make us behaviourally different to others.

Our frustration and sometimes difficulty with others in our team is quite often due to our behavioural preferences being different to theirs. I am sure like me, on occasion, you may have caught yourself inwardly thinking, "Why can't they be more like me?" or "If they did things the way

I did them, then it would make the job so much easier". Yes, let us be honest, we have all done this on occasion!

Ultimately, we all want success, however sometimes we achieve it in different ways.

So, let us explore the 2 attitudes and 4 functions in a bit more detail, however before we do, the last thing I would like to share with you is that when it comes to our psychological preferences, there is no right or no wrong, just difference.

Each preference has its strengths and equally its challenges. Ensuring that you and your colleagues in your team use all of them will help greatly in achieving success.

The attitudes: Introversion and Extraversion

Jung said that our attitude is the way in which we respond to situations and where we get our energy from, and he coined two well-known phrases to describe both attitudes: Introversion and Extraversion.

These 2 psychological preferences are the most frequent cause of misunderstanding, miscommunication, and frustration between individuals.

Both terms have their origins in Latin. "Intro" means within or inside and "extra" means outer or outside. "Vertere" is the Latin verb to turn. So, to get their behavioural energy, Introverts have a preference to turn within themselves, whilst Extraverts have a preference to turn outside of themselves.

You may sometimes see Extraversion spelled with an o, i.e. as Extroversion. Invariably, this will be in U.S. English texts, however in Latin there is no such word as "extro".

Those with a preference for Introversion primarily get their behavioural energy from within themselves, whilst those with a preference for Extraversion get their behavioural energy from interacting with others.

What is your preference?

Below are some phrases that are associated with Introversion and Extraversion. Read through them and make a note of the ones that resonate with you. The more you choose from one group over the other, the more of a preference you will have for that attitudinal function. If you end up with a reasonably close balance between the two, it is likely that you are what has been termed an Ambivert ("ambi" coming from the Latin, meaning both).

Below is a list of phrases and sentences that are associated with the attitude of Introversion:

- Having the reputation for being a good listener
- Being quiet
- Appearing shy
- Thinking before acting
- Having an inner focus
- Becoming drained by people
- Being reserved, shy or reflective
- Finding it difficult to express opinions in a large group
- Finding it uncomfortable being in the spotlight
- Preferring a small circle of friends
- Enjoying learning by observation
- Being able to concentrate for long periods of time
- Preferring to work in an environment with few distractions and little noise, enabling to concentrate on the task in hand
- Becoming quiet in larger groups
- Bottling up emotions

Below is a list of phrases and sentences that are associated with the attitude of Extraversion:

- Being loud
- Appearing confident
- Finding it comfortable to voice opinions in meetings
- Having an outer focus
- Become easily engaged in conversation, even with strangers
- Acting before they think
- Feeling energised by people
- Often being more comfortable working and generating ideas with a group rather than working alone
- Making friends easily
- Enjoying learning by doing
- Unloading their emotions
- May tend to dominate conversations
- Being easily distracted from what they are doing
- Needing to fill the silence
- Speaking first before thinking and sometimes regretting it

What each brings to a team

Introverted preference
Those with an Introverted preference often show a calm, self-contained and distant exterior, mentally absorbed in solving problems and analysing situations. Steady and reliable, they stick to rules and conventions. Self-sufficient and realistic, they are meticulous and painstaking in their attention to detail about people or tasks.

Extraverted preference
Those with an Extraverted preference often demonstrate an ability to spot possibilities and solutions. They prefer the excitement of the new, rather than the predictable. They are comfortable with working with many projects, people and situations, where they can see the results of their labour making a positive difference.

As can be seen, both preferences bring different, yet equally valuable skills to a team, so understanding these differences is a vital foundation upon which success is built. Failure to appreciate and value these different preferences may often result in negativity and frustration with those who are "not like me".

And remember, we can do both, but will have a preference for one over the other.

The 2 pairs of functions: Thinking and Feeling, and Sensing and Intuition

Jung noted 4 psychological functions: Thinking, Feeling, Sensing and Intuition. He said that they could either have an internal focus or Introverted attitude or an external focus, or Extraverted attitude.

Thinking and Feeling

Jung noted that with regards to our decision-making function, we have a preference for either Thinking or Feeling. Thinking is all about making decisions from an objective perspective, whereas Feeling is making decisions in a subjective way.

Sometimes people will use the word "think" or "feel" more than the other during a conversation, which may give you some clues about their preference.

Those with a preference for Thinking, you may catch saying, "Based on the data available, I think that this decision is the right one to make."

Those with a Feeling preference, you may catch saying, "Taking into account the needs of our customers, I feel this decision would work best for them."

Below is a list of phrases and sentences that are associated with the function of Thinking:

- Firm and rational
- Data driven
- Interested in logical analysis
- Makes decisions with the head
- Enjoys problem-solving
- Values factual decision-making
- Impersonal
- Analytical
- Spots logical inconsistencies
- Values truth and logic
- Objective

Below is a list of phrases and sentences that are associated with the function of Feeling:

- Caring, passionate and emotionally driven
- Dislikes conflict
- Interested in people and feelings
- Makes decisions with the heart
- Sensitive
- Struggles with telling the cold, hard truth
- Open to listening to others' viewpoints
- Empathic
- Values tact and diplomacy
- Relationship orientated
- Subjective

What each brings to a team

Thinking preference
Those with a preference for Thinking are good at analysing situations to seek out the truth. Because of this logical approach and objectivity, they are able to set aside emotions that may otherwise get in the way. They are able to present their findings with clarity. They are able to categorise and make sense of data from various sources and understand the links.

Feeling preference
Those with a preference for Feeling are good at picking up the nuances and subtleties of people's emotions and body language. They are sensitive to the needs of others and can often empathise with them, by putting themselves in their shoes. They will often seek out the fairest way to treat others when a decision has to be made, preferring to uphold harmony in relationships.

And once again, remember, we can do both, we just have a preference for one over the other.

Here's a real-life example that I hope brings these preferences to life for you.

I was working with a team that had an almost equal split of team members who had a preference for Thinking and Feeling, based on their personality profiles, which I had analysed prior to the individual and team development session that I was facilitating, to ensure that the learning was delivered in a way that met all their different needs.

There was discussion over a coffee break about how their company had told them that they needed to reduce the amount of parking spaces by 25%.

After the coffee break, I split the team into two groups, those with a Thinking preference and those with a Feeling preference, and asked them to discuss and agree three considerations about how to decide who should have a parking space after the 25% reduction.

Those with a Thinking preference came up with:

1. Obtaining data from HR based on seniority and length of service
2. Finding out the distance from work that people lived
3. Identifying those people who lived in the same area who could possibly car share

Those with a Feeling preference came up with:

1. Asking HR who had disabilities that required them to park in the car park
2. Finding out who had children of school age that they dropped off at school on their way to work
3. Undertaking a survey to find out how staff felt about the changes and asking for their suggestions

As you can see from this real-life example, both groups came at the problem from different perspectives.

In a team environment, therefore, it is ensuring that everyone appreciates these differences and that the team utilises these to obtain the best result, that takes into account both preferences.

Sensing and Intuition

Jung's second pair of functions is how we take in and process information and he named these Sensing and Intuition.

Those with a preference for Sensing, often known as Sensates, pay more attention to taking in information, yes, you have guessed it, using their five senses.

Those who have a preference for Intuition, or Intuitives, prefer to add a meaning or interpret information using patterns and possibilities.

Below is a list of phrases and sentences that are associated with the function of Sensing:

- Pay attention to physical reality, based on what they hear, see, touch, taste and smell
- Remember facts and details
- Like the practicality of learning things
- Follow patterns that are familiar
- Can repeat something said precisely
- Past and present orientated
- Very practical
- Take a common-sense approach
- Seek the truth
- Use their past experiences which work

Below is a list of phrases and sentences that are associated with the function of Intuition:

- Can repeat something said, however using different words
- Seek the idea behind the information
- May have a random train of thought
- Will frequently come up with unusual solutions or ideas
- Imagine the future and possibilities
- Create the big picture and understandings from little data
- See connections
- Inspired by ideas that spark their imagination
- Have a gut feel for doing the right thing
- Conceptual

What each brings to a team

Sensing preference

Those with a preference for Sensing are good when it comes to facts, figures and data. They will often move forward with a task in a methodical, step-by-step way, using their past experience of what works to guide and help them. When it comes to undertaking tasks, Sensates are very practical.

Intuition preference

Intuitives are future orientated and enjoy creating goals, the big picture, possibilities, and connections with other aspects of work. They enjoy generating ideas on how to do things, using their imagination to create the future. They enjoy working at a conceptual high level.

And once again, remember, we can do both, but just have a preference for one over the other.

I had the opportunity of working with a manufacturing company that had recently successfully diversified their product range and offerings to their customers. As part of the work that I had undertaken with them, the members of their teams had been profiled and they had been able to identify those individuals who had a strong preference for both Intuition and Sensing.

They had utilised the strengths of the Intuitives to come up with the ideas and concepts for the future product range and then utilised the strengths of the Sensates to identify those that would work and how they could practically bring them to the marketplace.

It was a great example of how to appreciate and utilise the strengths of both preferences.

Turning psychological preferences into colourful behaviours

The greatest gift that I received, in my early days as a leader, was my behavioural profile, as it enabled me to understand my strengths, my challenges, and how I communicated and made decisions.

This helped me realise not everyone was like me, and that to get the best from others I had to adapt my style in order to meet their needs.

The real magic happened when I enabled all my team to have their own behavioural profiles and I was able to understand both myself and others in the team better. I encouraged everyone in my team to share their profiles with each other.

The result of doing this was incredible. Our team now understood each other better, and in doing so, valued and appreciated what each of us brought to the team and, equally, those areas of challenge that each of us had.

We used our profiles on a regular basis, helping us to make decisions more effectively, communicate in a way that met the needs of everyone, play to people's strengths and come up with practical ideas that would make us more effective. Overall, the positive impact on how we worked as a team was quite extraordinary.

Now, there are many different profiling tools that are available to use, and I am not here to tell you which one to use. It may be that your company already uses a particular type.

However my personal view, based on my experience, coupled with feedback from clients, is that profiles that bring the psychology to life using colours are the ones that are the easiest to remember and are therefore used for a longer period of time, and on a more regular basis.

Most use the psychology of Jung, overlaying his psychological model with a colour model of human behaviour. Whilst the psychology underpinning these profiles is deep and complex, the use of colours makes it easy to understand, accessible to all, long-lasting, and provides a foundation of colourful language of human behaviour that can be used effectively both in work and home. It is about you and how you behave, how you perceive others and indeed how they perceive you.

In addition, the colours are a great way of keeping things positive in a team, as rather than possibly being seen as making a critical comment about an individual, you are able to use the colours to ensure that the observation you are making is about a particular behavioural style being exhibited and is not a personal attack.

As an example, you might say, "So how can we use our Red energy to agree the action that we need to take?" as opposed to saying, "We've spent too much time talking about things and we're no further forward."

When I facilitate development with teams or speak at conferences, I often start off by giving people a set of four coloured cards with different adjectives on them. I then ask them to be honest with themselves and to put the cards in order, based on how strongly they relate to the different adjectives.

So their top card will be the one with the most adjectives that they resonate with, down to the one at the bottom being the one with the adjectives that least resonate with them.

Let us have a look at the adjectives associated with these 4 high-level, colourful behavioural preferences.

On a good day

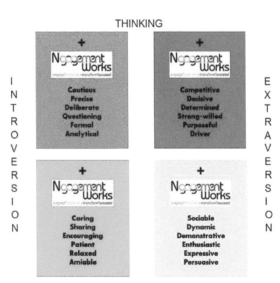

Hopefully, having read the above adjectives, you will have also completed this exercise, putting them into the order that resonates with you. It could be Blue, Green, Red, Yellow or maybe Yellow, Green, Blue, Red or another combination.

The important thing to always remember is that we are a mixture of **ALL** 4 behavioural preferences. We use them all, however some are stronger than others and we are more comfortable in using these styles and do so more often.

It does not mean that you are unable to connect and use the style that is least like you. It just means that this is not your preferred style and when you use it, you will find that it drains you of energy more quickly than when using one of your stronger preferences and styles.

As an example, my order for a long time was Yellow, Green, Red, Blue.

Blue (Introverted Thinking) was my least preferred style, however it did not mean that I could not use it. I was capable of writing in-depth costed proposals. I could analyse my accounts; I could focus on one thing that I was doing.

What it did mean, with Blue energy being my least preferred style, was that I did not enjoy doing these things. My coping mechanism for having to undertake anything that required a high degree of Blue energy was to either do it first thing in the morning to get it out of the way, or, wherever possible, ask someone with a lot of Blue energy to support me to complete the task, and play to their strengths.

You may have noticed that this *was* my colour order; now it has changed to Yellow, Green, Blue, Red, as we can and do change our behavioural preferences during our lives, based on the jobs we undertake and our experiences in life. Jung called this Individuation.

Whether you are leading a team or part of a team, it is of huge benefit to understand not only your behavioural preferences, but also the different styles of your colleagues, as in doing so you can play to each other's strengths, whilst supporting each other's challenges.

Now, if you are still a bit unsure of the order of your preferences, a way in which you can double check is to review the adjectives that are associated with having a bad day or being under stress.

On a bad day

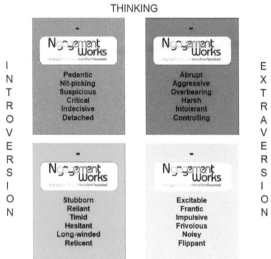

THINKING

	THINKING		
I N T R O V E R S I O N	Pedantic Nit-picking Suspicious Critical Indecisive Detached	Abrupt Aggressive Overbearing Harsh Intolerant Controlling	E X T R A V E R S I O N
	Stubborn Reliant Timid Hesitant Long-winded Reticent	Excitable Frantic Impulsive Frivolous Noisy Flippant	

FEELING

So hopefully you will have been able to reconfirm the order of your behavioural preferences and colours.

Now, you may be thinking, "Where are Sensing and Intuition?"

Well, these invariably will be taken into account in good profiling tools, however what I have shared is a high-level entry point to the colours and associated behaviours.

So, let us have a look at a summary of the characteristics of each of the 4 colours in the working environment.

Complementary styles

Due to the different behavioural preferences associated with each of the colours, the opposite preferences complement each other: Red and Green and Yellow and Blue.

As an example, and this was before I understood behaviours and colours, when I first became a project manager, I now know that I led with Yellow, followed by Green, then Red, then Blue.

So, leading with Yellow, I was extremely enthusiastic and positive about the benefits that the project I was leading would bring. My Green helped me connect with people, bringing me satisfaction that my project would be creating a new future for staff that would make their roles more fulfilling.

Not long after I had started my role, having undertaken an internal project management accreditation, I was asked to deliver a presentation to the heads of department about the project.

With that Yellow energy, that also enjoys verbal communication, I jumped at the chance. I wholeheartedly threw myself into creating a presentation with lots of visuals that would bring the project to life.

On the morning of the presentation, I had a quick run-through of the slides and watched as about 40 heads of department filed into the lecture theatre.

Once they had settled, I began my presentation with lots of energy, skipping from one slide to the next and explaining it, as most of them, as I mentioned, had lots of visual imagery. I enthused them, or so I thought, about how the project would help our people.

I was delighted that my timings were spot on, finishing with enough time for a quick Q&A session.

That is when things began to go wrong for me. What I had done was to create a presentation that ultimately appealed to those who were behaviourally like me, leading with Yellow, then Green energy.

One of the heads of department put up their hand to ask a question. I nodded for him to go ahead.

"This project is all well and good, however, as our departments will be footing the bill for it, I would like to understand the business benefits, timelines, costs and risks in more detail, as I am sure many of my colleagues in the room would." Nods of heads, some clapping and "Hear, hear" rippled around the auditorium.

It was at this point that I wanted the ground to open and swallow me up. What I was being asked, which all these years later is now plainly obvious to me, was a question from someone who led with my opposite preferences, Red and Blue energy.

Quickly thinking on my feet, so as to not lose any more face, I let everyone know that those details would be sent within the next week, directly to each of them, as they were not quite ready to share with them at the present time.

With my tail between my legs, I went back to my project team, letting them know what had been asked for. With that, one of my team said, "Not a problem, give me half a day and I will finish off putting that information together as I had almost completed it, however you never asked for it."

In that moment I had found my wing person, so to speak. Again, I did not realise at the time that the team were my behavioural opposite and up until that point, I had not really appreciated how much I needed them and how much we complemented each other, as they liked working in the background, whereas I was happy to stand up in front of people and be the spokesperson for the project team.

That cringeworthy lesson in how not to do it stuck with me over the years and when I learnt more about behaviours and colours and was able to create my own teams, whether it be a project or operational team, I always ensured that I had team members who complemented my style and strengths so that I did not end up putting together a homogeneous team made up of those with similar behavioural preferences to me.

It also taught me another lesson. By default, we all communicate in our own style, which ultimately, based on the 4 colour preferences, is only likely to be received well by about 50% of people, those with their top 2 behavioural colour energies that are the same as ours.

So now, whenever I communicate, whether via email, or face to face, I am always asking myself the question, "What have I included that will resonate with those who lead with Red, Blue, Green or Yellow energy?" You will notice that I think about it in the reverse of my colour preferences, so I focus on the ones that I struggle with first and foremost.

So, have I covered benefits, timescales, top-level plans and who to contact for those who lead with Red energy?

Have I got enough detail, covered risks, shared costs and where to obtain further information for those who lead with Blue energy?

Have I shared how it will impact on people or customers and the support available for those who lead with Green energy?

And finally, have I made it exciting and positive, explaining future opportunities and how to get involved, for those who lead with Yellow energy?

In doing so, I stand a much better chance that my communication will be received and importantly understood by a far greater number of people, than if I just use my natural style.

So, two learning points from the above, if you are creating a team, ensure the team are not behaviourally similar to yourself, as heterogeneous teams have a much greater chance of success.

Secondly, when communicating, think about the needs of others and "Do unto others as **THEY** would be done unto".

LEARNING WITH LAUGHTER

Having spoken at hundreds of conferences, I have always ensured that I deliver what the delegates have told me they want from a speaker. This is the reason why I have been given the moniker of "Mr. Infotainment", as based on feedback from delegates, they want a speaker to deliver information and learning in an entertaining way.

Having introduced the colour behavioural model, one of the ways that I add a bit of light-hearted entertainment and laughter is to share with them which of the four behavioural colours makes the greatest lover.

I let them know that in equal first place are all four colours.

Those who lead with Yellow energy make the greatest lovers as they are open to new ideas and are passionate.

Those who lead with Green energy make the greatest lovers as it is all about meeting your needs and ensuring you enjoy yourself.

Those who lead with Blue energy make the greatest lovers as they do it, and do it again and again, until it is just right.

And those who lead with Red energy make the greatest lovers, as they will tell you that it is happening at 9.30 pm and if you are not ready, they will start without you.

And afterwards, they all have a different reaction.

Those who lead with Yellow energy will say, "Wow, that was amazing, when are we going to do it again?"

Those who lead with Green energy will say, "How was it for you?"

Those who lead with Red energy will say, "I was good, wasn't I?"

And those who lead with Blue energy will say, "Please would you complete this feedback form."

I hope that the above has put a smile on your face; after all, life is too short to take ourselves and life too seriously!

My suggestion, based on what I have explained about behavioural preferences, is if you do not already, consider investing in profiles for you and your team so that everyone can value and appreciate these differences.

The key to ensuring that you maximise the return on your investment is to use a highly-regarded profiling tool and secondly, spend time with your team, using the knowledge and experience of a facilitator who understands the profile and is able to deliver individual and team development learning on how to practically use it.

Over the years, I have heard some horror stories where teams have not done the above and wasted their investment and indeed ended up doing more damage than good.

Finally, remember that behavioural profiles will never be 100% accurate, however if individuals have been honest about who they are when completing the evaluator to produce them, they often are 85%+ accurate. They are then an excellent way to open up conversations between team members about their behavioural preferences and styles and also to support personal development.

XYZ Team Colours

	Blue	Green	Yellow	Red			
Alex	21	55	75	96			
Brenda	66	14	69	79			
Colin	39	11	94	90			
Dawn	26	36	84	73			
Ethan	38	75	93	34			
Faith	27	55	89	31			
George	35	75	63	60			
Heather	71	87	31	49			
Ian	87	71	47	29			
Jane	81	65	36	39			
Karl	91	61	30	41			
Leanne	81	37	36	59			
TEAM	55	53	62	57			

I hope that I have provided you with a good understanding of the benefits of knowing **WHO** is in your team, both from a technical and behavioural skills perspective, and got you thinking about how to utilise both to help you and your team achieve even greater success.

Now, let's explore **HOW** effective your teamwork is.

CHAPTER 3:

HOW EFFECTIVE IS YOUR TEAMWORK?

The second part of this book focuses on providing you with a better understanding of **HOW** effective your teamwork may be.

There are 16 chapters, one for each of the 16 Elements which make up the Team DyNAmics Model that I created which is used by teams to measure how effective their teamwork is.

The model itself is explained in Chapter 4, prior to each of the 16 chapters about each of the Elements.

Before you start reading each chapter, I thought it would be beneficial to explain their structure.

POEM

In each chapter, I have included a verse of a poem that relates to the Element. You can also find the whole 16 verses of the poem near the end of the book.

CATEGORY

There are 4 top-level categories in the Team DyNAmics Model. Each has 4 Elements associated with it. The categories are Strategic Action (Red), Coactive Connections (Green), Framework Mapping (Blue) and Creative Interactions (Yellow). The Elements are colour-coded, so you know which 4 Elements relate to the 4 top-level categories.

Additionally, in the top corner of each page, you will see the infographic that relates to each Element, so that if you want you can easily navigate to an Element you are looking for.

TEAM DYNAMICS DEFINITION

An explanation of what the Element is about.

ETYMOLOGY

Often, we do not know the actual meaning of a word that we use on a regular basis and, in my experience, understanding which language the word originated from, and its original meaning, can add value in our understanding of how we use it today. This section will do that.

NEWBIE AND JULES

At the beginning of each chapter, you will come across a brief bit of dialogue between two characters, Newbie and Jules.

I am sure, like me, that you have come across people that inspire you and maybe who you aspire to be like.

For me, it was Julie, a leader who I was fortunate to work closely with during my time with Barclays. Julie had the ability to lead with what I call emotional strategy. She had this wonderful ability to deliver what was required strategically, whilst connecting emotionally with her team who were required to deliver the strategy.

Julie had a positive can-do attitude and was able to communicate strategy in a way that individuals connected with. She did not, however, shy away from tough decisions and giving people bad news but this was always delivered in an empathic way. She also had a wicked sense of humour, when and where appropriate.

Sadly, Jules passed away tragically a few years ago, well before her time. As a memory of the many things that she taught me and that I will always be grateful for, I have included some of our interactions that are relevant to the chapter they are in.

My affectionate name for Julie was Jules, and she called me Newbie, as I was the newest member of her team. I can hear her Scottish accent calling me this as I am writing.

WHAT IS...

This describes my thoughts in more detail as to what the Element represents.

BENEFITS

I have included 4 benefits, as examples of the positive impact that each Element has on other Elements in the model.

RED FLAGS

I have included 4 red flags, as examples that the Element may not be working as well as it should.

THE STORY

These are real-life stories relating to each Element, to bring it to life. The only changes to what actually happened relate to anonymity of individuals, teams or companies.

THE SUGGESTION

I have included a suggestion that you may wish to consider, if you feel that your team could benefit from using it. As mentioned previously, it is only a suggestion, due to the uniqueness of your team, in terms of who is in it and the environment that you work in.

FOOD FOR THOUGHT

These are 4 questions that will get you thinking about the Element and how it may relate to your teamwork.

CAPTURING THE PING MOMENTS

I hope that as you read this book you will have ideas that suddenly ping into your head, and it is important that you do not forget them. So, at the end of each chapter, I have included some free space for you to write down your ideas, so that you can then reflect and consider whether they are worthwhile sharing with your team.

CHAPTER 4:

THE TEAM DYNAMICS MODEL

*"Great teamwork doesn't just happen,
it happens in teams that work at being great."*

Nick Fewings
TEAMOLOGIST

What you have read so far, using the analogy of cooking, are the base ingredients upon which to achieve high-performance teamwork, knowing who is in your team, both from a behavioural/people and technical skills perspective.

This second part explores 16 Elements of teamwork, all important in helping to achieve high-performance teamwork, however, as with a recipe, some you may need to focus more on and some less on. This will be dependent on what is working well and not so well in your team.

Before we delve into each of the 16 Elements, it is important that you have an understanding of the history relating to why and how I created the Team DyNAmics Model.

I have always been curious about people and life in general and my wife often says, "You are always questioning things." She is right, I do. It may be for clarification, for more information, to learn more or a combination of all these.

I have always been curious, and this curiosity extended to teamwork when part of a team and also, when part way through my 21 years working for Barclays Bank, I was asked to lead my first ever team. As I've mentioned previously, from being a technical expert in a team, one day someone had the bright idea of promoting me to lead a team.

This was a huge shock for me. From pretty much having to look after myself and achieve my goals and responsibilities and play my part in the end-to-end processes of the team I was in, now I had to lead a team, ensuring that they were motivated, inspired, and worked effectively to achieve team goals, whilst also developing as individuals.

And as is sadly still the case today, some 30 years later, a lot of people just like me are promoted to lead a team without any formal training in how to lead that team effectively. A case of sink or swim.

I hold my hand up; in my early years of leadership, even though I had been part of a team and was curious about teamwork, I made many mistakes and no doubt upset many individuals on my team with my ineptitude when it came to leadership. I take this opportunity to apologise unreservedly to those who had to experience this.

My leadership skills became better when I studied behavioural psychology, providing me with an understanding and appreciation of behavioural diversity in team members. Who were the quiet ones? Who were the loud ones? Who made decisions, based around relationships and harmony? Who made decisions based on logic, data and information? Who preferred to work in a quiet part of the office? Who needed to be in the thick of it, surrounded by their colleagues and a degree of noise and banter?

As mentioned previously, I also enhanced my knowledge of people by becoming accredited to use a colourful model of human behaviour based on the psychology of Carl Jung, the Swiss psychologist. Every team I led thereafter, I invested in having the individuals in the team profiled.

I have used behavioural profiling ever since when facilitating team development with my clients, providing them with a vital tool to understand **WHO** is in their team from a behavioural perspective.

In addition to behavioural profiling, I also ensured everyone knew the technical skills of their colleagues, gleaned from their CVs, HR records, certificates of achievement and talking to them.

To this day, it still worries me that many leaders and indeed teams do not know **WHO** is in their team, from both a behavioural/people and technical skills perspective. Hopefully, having read the first part of this book, you will now have a better understanding of the importance of both.

However, knowing **WHO** is in your team only provides half the solution. You also need to know **HOW** effectively individuals are working together as a team.

In my first leadership role, as part of my daily walkabouts and chats with different members of my team, I would individually ask them questions about their performance, successes they had had or challenges they faced. Invariably, those individual conversations spilled over into many aspects of teamwork, as their individual jobs were part of the bigger picture of what the team was there to achieve.

So my natural curiosity continued during our regular team meetings, as I started asking the whole team questions about their teamwork. I would keep a note of those questions that resulted in good discussion, in that the question highlighted a strength or indeed a challenge that the team faced, that needed to be explored further to find a practical solution that we agreed to implement.

Over the years, I led various teams, and I added to my initial shortlist of questions and also made slight amendments to the ones I had used to make them more effective. Those that did not work, I discarded.

It got to the point where I had created a set of 48 questions that covered different aspects of teamwork. One day, I sat down and began to group these questions into what I called Elements. There were 16 Elements, each with 3 questions. I then created an appropriate name for each of these 16 Elements of teamwork.

One day, whilst out walking my dog Zippo, time which I called my "Ideas Cooker" as it enabled me to "cook" the ideas I had thought about, testing them out in my head as to whether they were worth progressing further, I was thinking about these 16 Elements and I had an epiphany.

I suddenly realised that each of the 16 Elements fell into one of the 4 behavioural colour preferences in the profiling tool that I was using, and that they were evenly distributed, 4 Elements for each colour.

I called this higher level grouping Categories. So, 48 questions, 16 Elements, 4 Categories, which became the Team DyNAmics Model.

It is no accident that I called it Team DyNAmics, with a capital DNA. Teams are dynamic, people moving in and out of the team on a regular basis, including leaders. In doing so, they have an impact on how the team behaves and performs. In addition, both internal and external factors will have an impact on team performance and need to be monitored, to understand the effect that these may have.

Just like the DNA within us is unique to us, so the DNA of a team is unique to that team. As changes occur in terms of team members and also what the team needs to achieve, then so too its DNA changes.

To support high-performance teamwork, being able to measure, and in doing so understand this DNA, enables both leaders and teams to understand those things in their team's DNA that are positive and working well, and also equally importantly understand areas that are causing the team challenges and need to be addressed and changed.

What I needed now was a logo to represent the model and provide people with an understanding of it, and then in September 2015, the idea for the logo came to me and two strange coincidences followed thereafter, that made me realise that the logo was meant to be.

As a kid, I absolutely loved Spirograph. I would pin the plastic outer circle design that I had chosen to the paper and into the cardboard supplied. I would then choose the inner circular designs and appropriate felt-tip pen to create a design.

There were many frustrating occasions when I had not secured the pins sufficiently and part way through creating my design, a pin would come loose, resulting in the wheel I was using shooting across the paper and ruining my design.

Irrespective of these disasters, I loved Spirograph and made many different designs over the years, colouring many of them in so that the patterns and colours were symmetrical.

Near my birthday a few years ago, I decided to relive my youth and buy Spirograph. Not much had changed over the years, apart from the fact that there were, probably due to health and safety, no pins, which also meant no cardboard. Instead of pins, the circular wheels are now attached by white-tack.

No sooner had my gift to myself arrived than I was at the dining room table creating my first design.

I used the four primary colours found in the colour model of behaviours, being red, yellow, green and blue. I looked at what I had created and bang, the idea for the Team DyNAmics logo leapt off the page at me.

I later found out that what I had drawn was very similar to a design that has appeared throughout most civilisations, throughout the ages, something I now know is called the Flower of Life.

Then the first of two coincidences occurred.

THE COLDPLAY COINCIDENCE

Coldplay are one of my favourite bands. I know for a lot of people they are a Marmite band; you either like them or hate them. Well, I am firmly in the former camp.

One of the best live concerts I have ever been to was in June 2012, when I saw them perform at the Emirates Stadium, London, on the UK leg of their Mylo Xyloto Tour.

One of my favourite albums of theirs is *A Head Full Of Dreams*, released in December 2015. When it came out, the logo just hit me between the eyes, due to its similarity to the Team DyNAmics logo that I had created.

It was created by Pilar Zeta, an artist and graphic designer who grew up in Buenos Aires, Argentina. She worked closely with the group to create the album cover, which features in the centre a design of circles called the Flower of Life.

In Pilar's words, "The Flower of Life has existed for thousands of years. It's a pattern that's in nature. If you grab a leaf and multiply it, then it creates the Flower of Life. It's on the walls of the Osiris temple in Egypt. And it is a very beautiful shape because it is made with circles, and it is a nice representation of connection and the whole. So, we had this idea of the Flower of Life with the colours."[2]

THE FORBIDDEN CITY COINCIDENCE

The second coincidence, when I investigated the Flower of Life further, was finding out that one of the cultures that used it was the emperors of the Ming and Qing dynasties, who lived in the Forbidden City in Beijing, China. The Flower of Life is found in spherical form underneath the paw of the "fu-dog", more accurately known as the guardian lion. They were considered to be the guardians of knowledge.

In June 2017, I was invited to be a keynote speaker at a leadership conference in Beijing. I presented on leading and developing high-performance teamwork and as part of my presentation, I shared my Team DyNAmics Model.

A few days later, one of the cultural visits was to the Forbidden City, in the centre of Beijing, which was the home of the imperial rulers of China. It was commissioned in 1406 and first occupied in 1420.

The site was designated a UNESCO World Heritage Site in 1987. Whilst some of the buildings in the complex have been rebuilt, having been destroyed in wars, a lot of the buildings, whilst restored, are mainly original. It is truly a remarkable place to visit.

As I wandered around the city, marvelling at the incredible and numerous palace buildings and temples, I turned a corner and could not believe my eyes. There, in front of one of the Imperial Palace buildings, was a huge statue of a fu-dog, and underneath one of its paws was a spherical Flower of Life.

The fu-dog is a traditional feng shui symbol of protection. They were often sculpted with a raised paw resting on a spherical representation of the Flower of Life, as shown in the photo that I took.

The final stage of creating the Team DyNAmics logo was to add the symbols that represent the 16 Elements around the outside of the design.

As you may have noticed, each leaf that represents one of the 16 Elements overlaps with others. This recognises that each Element interplays with others and often a change in one of the Elements will have a knock-on effect on a number of other Elements.

Because of this, it is no good just focussing on one Element; each needs to be given attention, to ensure that they are working as effectively as possible and in harmony with each other. Let me explain.

THE RIPPLE EFFECT

Imagine you are at the edge of a lake. It is a calm, warm day and the water in the lake is like glass. Imagine picking up a pebble and tossing it high into the air above you. You watch as it descends and hits the water with a loud plop.

Ripples begin to emanate from the point at which the pebble hit the water.

The ripples nearest where the pebble has dropped are the biggest and as the circle of ripples disperses from the centre, whilst they become wider in circumference, they get smaller, until they eventually disappear.

It is the same with the 16 Elements of the model, in that there are some Elements that have a stronger impact on team performance, if they are not working as well as they should.

The following chapters are in order of their importance, hence starting with Purpose and ending with Transformation, going left to right from top to bottom as shown in the diagram below. This is only my opinion, based on my knowledge and experience of using the model. Do not therefore feel that you have to read each chapter in order. If there is an Element that you know is an issue for you and your team, then go right to that chapter.

Team DyNAmics

	Strategic Action	Coactive Connection	Framework Mapping	Creative Interactions
Level 1	Purpose	Trust	Planning	Collaboration
Level 2	Accountability	Commitment	Roles & Skills	Communication
Level 3	Decision-Making	Team Meetings	Processes	Environment
Level 4	Vision	Diversity	Reflection	Transformation

MEASURING YOUR TEAM EFFECTIVENESS

"If you don't measure how effective your teamwork is, how do you know how good you are or what you could achieve?"

As mentioned, most teams measure their success via KPIs (Key Performance Indicators), however their performance against these is a by-product of how effectively they are working as a team.

Say, for instance, that your team is achieving 75% of your KPIs, so doing reasonably well. What if you measured your team effectiveness and found out that this was 65%? Just think about the positive impact this would have on your KPIs, if you got your team effectiveness up to 80%!

The Team DyNAmics Model enables teams to measure their overall team effectiveness and the effectiveness of the 16 Elements that make up the model, using anonymous feedback from team members, based on completing an online questionnaire and producing an eight-page Team DyNAmics Report.

It enables a team to understand whether they are challenged, average or high performing, in terms of their teamwork. This enables them to celebrate and continue to use their strengths, whilst having focussed discussions about those areas of their teamwork that need to be changed.

Team DyNAmics can be re-run, at an appropriate future date, after any agreed changes have been implemented by the team, to understand the impact the changes have had as a process of continuous improvement.

The diagram on the following page, shows an example summary page from a Team DyNAmics Report.

It shows how many team members responded to the questionnaire.

The overall team effectiveness, based on their amalgamated responses.

The ranking of the 16 Element and the percentage effectiveness of each.

The percentage effectiveness of the 4 Categories, into which each of the 16 Elements are grouped, 4 per Category.

Subsequent pages of the report, include lower level reporting of team members responses, including the maximum and minimum score given to any of the 48 statements, the average score, spread of scores and ranking of individual statements, out of 48.

N.B. Individual team member responses remain anonymous.

Team DyNAmics Excerpt

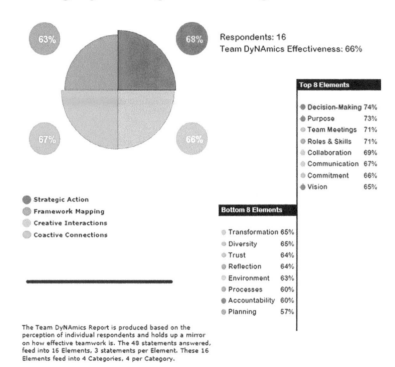

Category Average Percentage

Respondents: 16
Team DyNAmics Effectiveness: 66%

63%
68%
67%
66%

- Strategic Action
- Framework Mapping
- Creative Interactions
- Coactive Connections

Top 8 Elements

- Decision-Making 74%
- Purpose 73%
- Team Meetings 71%
- Roles & Skills 71%
- Collaboration 69%
- Communication 67%
- Commitment 66%
- Vision 65%

Bottom 8 Elements

- Transformation 65%
- Diversity 65%
- Trust 64%
- Reflection 64%
- Environment 63%
- Processes 60%
- Accountability 60%
- Planning 57%

The Team DyNAmics Report is produced based on the perception of individual respondents and holds up a mirror on how effective teamwork is. The 48 statements answered, feed into 16 Elements, 3 statements per Element. These 16 Elements feed into 4 Categories, 4 per Category.

The Team DyNAmics Effectiveness percentage represents the overall perception of how effective teamwork is.

Based on my experience of those teams that have used the Team DyNAmics Model to measure their overall team effectiveness, those who score below 65% are challenged, between 65–84% are average, and those scoring 85% and above are high performing.

So, now you know more about the Team DyNAmics Model, let's have a look at the first of the 16 Elements, being Purpose.

CHAPTER 5:

PURPOSE:
ELEMENT 1 OF 16

*"Understanding our **Team Purpose** is where we must begin,*
What this enables and the benefits it will bring.
For this will keep us all on track, give focus to what we do,
Ensuring everything delivered adds positive value."

Category: Strategic Action

Team DyNAmics Definition: The understanding of what your team exists to do, what this enables and the benefits this delivers.

Etymology: From Old French, meaning intention or aim.

Newbie: *What is the point of having a Team Purpose?*
Jules: *Team Purpose is the point.*

WHAT IS PURPOSE?

*"Team Purpose provides focus,
understanding, clarity and unity."*

I believe that Team Purpose is the most important area of teamwork to get right. You may read other books about teamwork that suggest it is trust. Let me explain my rationale.

Think about when you have applied for a job. Initially, have you applied for the job because you know the team members trust each other? Probably not; you apply for the job as it interests you and you think that you have the skills, knowledge and experience to do it.

In the past, I have been asked if I would join a particular team, but have declined, as whilst I have known and trusted the individuals within the team, their team purpose has not inspired or motivated me enough to want to join them.

Similarly, think about project teams that are created. They are not created by simply getting together a group of people who trust each other. They are created based on the purpose or goals of the project and by putting together a team of individuals with the appropriate skills and experience to support the project goals being achieved.

Throughout my 30 years of leading and working with teams, individuals have regularly shared with me that having meaning in their working lives was an important factor. They wanted to understand how what they did in their role helped their team to achieve its goals.

Just think about how demoralising it would be if you were doing a job and you did not understand the reason why you were doing it, or how it added value to what everyone else in the team did.

Team Purpose enables an individual team member to understand how their role contributes to achieving the goals of the team and motivates them to complete their part of it to the best of their ability.

It never fails to surprise me how many teams that I work with do not have a clearly articulated Team Purpose that everyone in the team knows.

BENEFITS

1. It provides a common understanding across the whole of the team and can be shared with new team members as part of their induction, thus supporting **Commitment** to the team. In addition it can be used to attract new team members.
2. It helps individuals to understand what part their **Role** plays and how their **Skills** can be utilised to best effect, to ensure the goals set for the team are achieved.
3. It creates a foundation upon which a **Vision** of the future can be created, that the team aspires to achieve.
4. It ensures that any ideas put forward to help the **Transformation** of the way the team works are aligned with the Team Purpose.

RED FLAGS

1. Individuals do not align their role with the purpose or goals of the team and will therefore do things that they feel are important to them, as opposed to the team.
2. Personal success is more important than team success. Individuals focus more on delivering tasks, milestones or goals that provide them with a tick in the box.
3. Team members have different perspectives as to what needs to be done.
4. Collaboration and knowledge sharing are infrequent. A silo mentality occurs: individuals looking after themselves and not really interested in helping others, nor indeed sharing their knowledge, expertise or ideas.

THE STORY
The bean counters

In one of my first leadership roles, I was asked to lead an already established finance team. I had been made aware that they had low esteem about what they did and the value it added to the organisation.

Their perception of the team was mirrored in the business areas that they had working relationships with. They were known as the "bean counters", which had become a self-fulfilling prophecy and reinforced the low self-esteem that the team members had of their team.

At the first meeting I had with the team, I asked each of them to write down, individually, *"What does our team exist to do?"* Once they had done this I asked them, one by one, to read out what they had written.

It was little surprise to me that ten different statements were shared. Their responses were not just a little bit different, however; they varied considerably, which was deeply worrying.

Eventually, after discussing their different perspectives, they agreed that one person's statement was probably the best. This was *"To produce monthly accounts that are as accurate as possible as quickly as possible after month-end"*.

I am sure that you would agree that this is pretty boring and did not instil a sense of pride in what the team did, nor indeed motivate and inspire individuals to play their part in achieving it to the best of their ability. No wonder they felt bad about themselves and other parts of the business did not value what they did either.

So, I set about facilitating a session that would result in the creation of a new Team Purpose Statement that would make them feel positive about the work they did and the value that it added to other parts of the business.

For the next couple of hours, I challenged them and their perception as to what the team existed to do. I did this by getting them to focus on agreeing three fundamental parts that together would make a clear, motivational and compelling Team Purpose Statement, that they would have collectively created and agreed and therefore buy into.

Eventually, after many ideas and much discussion, the team came up with a Team Purpose Statement that they all agreed upon.

This is what they came up with:

The Finance Team exists to ensure the timely delivery of value-adding financial and accounting data, and key performance indicators to our global business units, enabling them to make informed investment decisions, that deliver tangible benefits to our customers, staff and company.

The team loved what they had collectively created and felt a sense of pride and ownership. We then began to share it with others and took every opportunity to make others aware of it, via our newsletters, bulletins, emails, noticeboards and indeed on the front of the monthly information pack that was created and sent to our global business units.

Within about six weeks, the perception of other departments had changed significantly, as they too realised the value-adding service that the team delivered. This had a positive knock-on effect on individuals in the team and the team's overall morale increased significantly. The moniker of "the bean counters" was soon assigned to history.

THE SUGGESTION

It does not matter whether you are a leadership team, an operational team or a project team, Team Purpose is the most important of the 16 Elements that you need to create and commit to as a team, as it provides the foundation upon which high-performance teamwork is achieved, by giving focus to everything you do.

TEAM PURPOSE STATEMENT MODEL
Nick Fewings, Ngagementworks

CREATING A TEAM PURPOSE STATEMENT

The three parts to creating a Team Purpose Statement are as follows:

1. What does our team exist to do? What is it that we *really do and deliver?*
2. What does this enable to happen? What additional things does this really help us to do?
3. What are the resulting benefits? How do others really benefit from what we do?

THE PROCESS

1. Check out the understanding of your Team Purpose by getting team members to individually write down and then share what they think your team exists to do. This will give you a good idea as to whether there is consensus and similarity or whether there is disagreement and difference.
2. If the latter, agree a time to define your Team Purpose Statement. One hour should be a good starter.
3. Ensure as many of your team as possible are involved in creating it, to ensure buy-in and commitment.

4. Make sure it includes the three elements, DO, ENABLE and BENEFITS.

5. Keep it simple, no jargon or acronyms.

6. Allow a period of time for individuals to think about what has been created and discuss and agree any small changes, to polish it into a final version.

7. Get agreement from as many team members as possible, however definitely a majority, as to the final version.

8. Check it out with some people outside of your team, to see if they understand it.

9. Once created, ensure that you diarise to review it at least once a quarter, to ensure it is still relevant and valid and that everyone in your team understands it, especially those who may have joined the team in the interim.

If you do the above, the next time a person says to you, *"So tell me, what does your team do?"* your Team Purpose Statement should trip off your tongue with ease.

FOOD FOR THOUGHT

Q1. Knowing what you now know, what would you say that your Team Purpose was?

Q2. What would happen if you asked your team to individually write down what they thought your Team Purpose was? Would they all write the same as you, or would they write something different?

Q3. If a new person joined your team, as part of their induction, what would be the benefits to them of knowing what your Team Purpose was?

Q4. Based on your experience of how your team work currently, what benefits are there in spending time discussing and agreeing a Team Purpose Statement with them?

PING MOMENTS

Time to reflect on this chapter and capture
any ideas that it has given you.

_____

_____

_____

_____

_____

_____

_____

_____

_____

_____

_____

_____

_____

_____

_____

_____

CHAPTER 6:

TRUST:
ELEMENT 2 OF 16

*"**Trust** between each of us we must build deep and strong,*
To appreciate each other, so we can get along.
It's vital that we realise that we're stronger as a team,
If we're to work effectively and fulfil our dream."

Category: Coactive Connections

Team DyNAmics Definition: The emotional
bond that glues teams together.

Etymology: From Old Norse, meaning strong.

Newbie: How can I build trust with those in my team?
Jules: Firstly, by being authentic.

WHAT IS TRUST?

"Built over time, so easily shattered in a moment."

I believe that there are two levels of trust that apply to teams. I call these Organisational Trust and Appreciative Trust.

Organisational Trust is at a more superficial level and is about complying with organisational rules and regulations. Examples of these are:

- Being trusted not to steal company assets, such as laptops or stationery
- Not sharing intellectual property with competitors
- Turning up on time to do your job
- Complying with Health and Safety
- Not overstating overtime
- Changing passwords when required

Appreciative Trust goes much deeper and of the two is more important. Appreciative Trust is about individuals within the team appreciating each other for who they are, their background, their beliefs, their sexuality, their values, their fears and challenges.

Appreciative Trust enables an individual to wholly be themselves, without any judgement being made by other team members. It creates mutual respect.

Team members can open up about their feelings and emotions. They can share their challenges, knowing that other team members may be able to help them overcome them.

As a team, you need to create the right environment for Appreciative Trust between team members to flourish. You need them to do the right thing not only for themselves but for the good of the team overall.

Lack of trust ultimately destroys teams as they end up just being a group of individuals who look out for themselves, as opposed to looking out for each other.

BENEFITS

1. Individuals are happy to be held **Accountable** for their behaviours and actions, in the knowledge that any mistakes they make will be seen as a learning experience, and positive support will be freely given by others to help them develop.
2. **Team Meetings** become increasingly effective and efficient, as individuals are happy to share their views, thoughts, feelings and ideas, knowing that they will be listened to positively. They know that whilst their views, thoughts, feelings and ideas may be challenged, they will not be challenged personally.
3. Handover points between individuals in **Processes** occur smoothly, as there is trust that the person handing it over does so in a fit for purpose way, so that the next team member can complete their part of the process.
4. It assists the team in **Reflection**, as everyone knows that if they have an opinion, it will be listened to.

RED FLAGS

1. Team meetings lack energy, enthusiasm and ideas. There is a reticence from team members to share their thoughts or feelings, often fearful of being personally attacked by others.
2. Individuals seek permission before taking actions, which more often than not they do not need permission to undertake. This is a safeguarding mechanism, in case what they do causes an issue.
3. Individuals are not comfortable in delegating work to others, as they do not believe in their capability to achieve the standards that are expected.

4. Pointing the finger, gossiping or talking behind other team members' backs occurs frequently. This is often to ensure that any criticism is deflected from themselves onto others.

THE STORY
Life journey

Tania had recently been promoted within the team, to team leader. She had worked with me at a previous company and was keen to understand how effectively she and her team were working together.

She explained in a call what her team development objectives were and that she felt that the team were too focussed on tasks and did not devote enough time on building positive relationships with each other. She felt that this was having a detrimental effect on their teamwork and effectiveness.

As the team had all been profiled in a previous session that I had facilitated, after hearing what she had to say I suggested that she use the Team DyNAmics Model to measure the team's effectiveness and highlight their strengths and areas of challenge. Tania agreed.

On reviewing the Team DyNAmics Report, I noticed that Tania's feeling was correct, as Trust had been scored extremely low by the team.

I put together an appropriate learning programme to meet Tania's objectives and used the Team DyNAmics Report as a foundation to do so.

When we got to the part of the programme relating to Trust, I gave a sheet of flipchart paper and pen to each of the team members. I then asked them to draw a story of their life, including as much or as little information as they were prepared to share with the rest of their colleagues.

As they were doing this I wandered around the room, looking at the fascinating stories that they were creating.

After letting them know that the allotted 15 minutes was almost up, I gave them an opportunity to share their life stories.

Tania agreed to go first and began to share hers, which included several dark clouds on her timeline. She shared about her teenage life, her family and where she was brought up. How she had then gone on to university, secured her first job, got married and had the first of her two children.

It was at this point that she shared with her team that, following the birth of her son, she had suffered from post-natal depression and that bouts of depression had continued throughout her life since this time.

You could have heard a pin drop. Tania said, "I wanted to share this with you, so you know that when I'm not behaving normally, it may be because I am having one of my bouts of depression, so don't think that it is anything you have done personally."

One of the team shared that they had never known this and that they really appreciated Tania sharing this with them. The rest of the team also showed their appreciation of Tania's openness.

With that, one of the team asked if they could have another five minutes to add some further information to their story and the rest of the team agreed.

Because of Tania's openness, she had immediately created a safe environment for others in the team to feel comfortable sharing much more personal information about their lives.

Fast-forward six months, and when the team remeasured using the Team DyNAmics Model, their effectiveness scores had increased across all 16 Elements, with Trust increasing the most.

THE SUGGESTION

As trust takes time to develop between individuals, it is important that time is spent by the team in building it on a regular and continuous basis.

As I have mentioned, it is the development of Appreciative Trust that makes the biggest difference, so any activities should focus on this and enable individuals to open up about themselves, not only from a work perspective but more importantly from a personal point of view. This will allow colleagues to find out more about each other, enabling trust to develop both quicker and deeper.

One of the activities that I mentioned above, called "Life Journey", is a good place to start. Below are a couple of others that you may want to consider, that I have found work really well over the years.

An Unusual Fact

Each team member writes down their name and an unusual fact about themselves, that they may not have previously shared with their colleagues, on a piece of paper. A chairperson is assigned, who collects the pieces of paper in.

The chairperson then reads out the first unusual fact, at which point the other team members have to guess who it is about. After they have guessed, the person who wrote it owns up and then tells the backstory that relates to their unusual fact.

Quite often, this can reveal some amazing facts about individuals and over the years I have used it with teams, I have had people who have sung in front of the Pope, been on a hijacked plane, rung the bells at both St. Paul's Cathedral and Westminster Abbey, climbed Kilimanjaro, been in the Olympics, skydived and much more.

Similarities and Differences

For this, you will need about a dozen flipchart sheets. At the top of each one, write a title. For example, Favourite Food, Saddest Moment, Most Loved Holiday Destination, A Phobia, Band You Like, Best Concert You've Seen, How Many Operations You've Had, How Many Siblings You Have, Place of Birth.

The above are just a few examples that I have used and I am sure you can think of others. Ideally you want between 10 and 12 different themes, with a mixture of positives and also themes that allow individuals to share their vulnerabilities.

Once you have written them on the flipchart sheets, one per theme, put them up on the walls or find a suitable place where team members can write their comments on them.

Give each team member a pen and get them to write down their answers and put their name beside their answer.

Once everyone has completed this, then you can get everyone to review the sheets, one sheet at a time, and get into conversations about similarities and differences.

FOOD FOR THOUGHT

Q1. Why do you think that Trust is important if your team is to achieve its goals?

Q2. In what areas of your teamwork do you perceive that Trust could be better?

Q3. How could you build in time for your team to talk more openly about how they are thinking or feeling about their teamwork?

Q4. What could you do to help team members find out more about each other personally?

LEARNING THROUGH LAUGHTER

I was facilitating a team development session with an international team. They had come together from around the world and this was only the second time they had all been in the same room together. I decided to use the "Unusual Fact" activity that I shared above to get them to open up about themselves.

So I handed out pieces of paper, explained what they had to do and then collected in what they had written. I did this just before a coffee break and as the team left the room for refreshments, I checked what they had written.

I was shocked to see that one person, who I thought was being really honest and open, had written that "At the age of seven, I killed a man".

I had the opportunity to have a private word with the individual who had written it and asked if they were happy to share something as shocking. They smiled and told me that it was not a problem.

So, after the refreshment break, when all the team were back in the training room, I began to read out the unusual facts. There was a great amount of guessing and fascination at some of the backstories. Then it was time to read out the shocking fact.

"Someone in your team at the age of seven killed a man." Silence ensued and I saw the shock, yet fascination, on people's faces, as to who the fact belonged to.

After much guessing, Craig, who was based in Australia, owned up that it was him. He then revealed to all of us his backstory.

Craig was in the Cub Scouts when he was younger and on a regular, monthly basis, as part of their community work, they would visit an old people's home and spend time with the residents, most of whom were in their 70s and 80s.

Craig struck up a friendship with Frank, who at the time was 82. He and Frank would, weather permitting, sit outside on a bench and chat about what they had both done over the previous month.

Now the week before one of Craig's visits, it had been his seventh birthday. Frank knew this and had got him a card and a small present. They had then chatted about Craig's birthday, his presents, his party and what party food he had eaten.

With that, Craig explained that part way through his chat with Frank, one of the nursing staff tapped him on the shoulder and suggested that he come inside. As Craig got up from the bench that him and Frank had been sat upon, he looked over and it appeared Frank had fallen asleep. Unbeknown to Craig, Frank had actually peacefully passed away, listening to him, sitting in the sunshine on the bench.

The nursing staff thought it was a good idea to let his parents know, so when the Cub Scout Leader took Craig home, he came into their house and explained to his parents what had happened.

Unfortunately, Craig's teenage sister was listening in, and as siblings sometimes do, thought it highly amusing to tell family and friends that "Craig killed a man by chatting to him for too long".

Laughter erupted in the training venue from Craig's team members.

Whilst the way Craig recounted this unusual fact was extremely funny, there was a twist in the tale because for a number of years, Craig would not speak to anyone for more than ten minutes, in case he killed them!

PING MOMENTS

Time to reflect on this chapter and capture
any ideas that it has given you.

_____

_____

_____

_____

_____

_____

_____

_____

_____

_____

_____

_____

_____

_____

_____

_____

CHAPTER 7:

PLANNING:
ELEMENT 3 OF 16

*"**Plans** we need to put in place, so everybody knows,*
The steps we all need to take, so we achieve our goals.
Some revisions may be needed, as we all should know,
When changes sometimes happen that are out of our control."

Category: Framework Mapping

Team DyNAmics Definition: Knowing what
needs to be done, by whom and by when.

Etymology: From Latin, meaning level or flat surface.

Newbie: Why do we need a plan if we know our end goal?
Jules: So we know how much we have achieved
and how much we have left to do.

WHAT IS PLANNING?

"A plan needs to be a living document, regularly updated when changes occur. It is not something created annually and assigned to a drawer, never to see the light of day again."

Planning provides your team with a route map of where you need to get to, in order to achieve the goals set. It provides focus, so that neither your team, nor indeed individuals, go off in a different direction. It also provides an opportunity to set milestones of what needs to be achieved, by whom and by when.

Let us be honest, planning is often seen as a boring, yet necessary evil, something that is often given half-hearted attention and effort, essentially a required annual activity, often insisted on by the company. Something that involves a few people on the team is then shared with the whole of the team and then put to bed, never to see the light of day again.

You may have heard of the 7Ps, an adage of the British Army, which stands for Proper Planning and Preparation Prevents Piss Poor Performance, which is often adapted in business to omit the fifth P!!

Those teams who do not set aside sufficient time to create a plan to help them achieve their goals invariably fail. And, as you will read later in the chapter, it does not have to be a boring process.

Teams that take the approach of involving as many people in the team as possible in the planning process invariably achieve better results.

Involving the whole team supports individual commitment and buy-in to the plan and individual sense of ownership.

In addition, a good plan will provide guidance and direction for the team, help them to measure progress and understand what is left to be achieved.

In terms of setting goals, at an individual level, having a team plan makes it easier to create these, as individuals have clarity about the part that they play in helping the team achieve its goals.

BENEFITS

1. It binds the team to a common **Purpose**.
2. It helps creativity and idea generation, when **Transformation** is required, to overcome challenges.
3. It helps support **Accountability** at an individual level.
4. **Communication** is given a focus.

RED FLAGS

1. Deadlines are frequently missed, and future work is delayed.
2. Things go wrong on a regular basis, with individuals ending up doing things that feel right for them.
3. Duplication of effort occurs.
4. More time is spent on firefighting than moving forward positively.

THE STORY
Ten Tors

My first experience of the importance of planning, preparation and indeed teamwork occurred when I was fourteen, and a schoolboy at Devonport High School For Boys, the grammar school that I went to in Plymouth, my city of birth.

Starting in the 1960s and still continuing annually to this day, the Ten Tors Challenge, organised by the British Army, takes place on the Saturday and Sunday before the May Bank Holiday near Okehampton Army Camp, on the North Moor of Dartmoor National Park, Devon, UK.

The event was open to teams of six, from all over the UK. Due to the impact on the environment, it is now restricted to 2,400 individuals, and whilst it was open to competitors from around the globe, due to its popularity, it has now been restricted to teams from the South West of the UK.

It is a two-day trek on difficult, hilly terrain, with three different distances – 35, 45 or 55 miles – depending on the age of the team.

Teams of six are required to visit ten specified tors (a hill or rocky peak); on the top of each tor is a checkpoint. Each team is required to visit all of the specified checkpoints in order. Up to two members per team may fall out during the challenge.

There are four different routes, which are made all the more difficult by the fact that competitors have to carry everything they need with them.

Teams arrive at Okehampton Army Camp on the Friday before the hike, watch a safety briefing video and have their equipment checked, a thorough process known as scrutineering. Teams must carry all their food, clothing, tents, stoves, fuel, navigation equipment, maps, emergency rations and a first aid kit; they also collect drinking water from the moor and use water purification tablets. Each team has a nominated team leader, who is responsible for ensuring that the team's route card is stamped at each tor.

All the teams start at 07:00 on the Saturday from an area of flat land close to Okehampton Camp on the northern edge of Dartmoor. They stand in a semicircle and set off when a cannon fires. They have 34 hours to visit each of the ten tors on their route in the correct order.

Teams must not pass through a checkpoint between 22:00 on Saturday and 06:00 on Sunday morning, nor may they pass the eighth tor until the Sunday. Those on 35-mile routes must camp at one of the manned tors on their route, while 45 and 55-mile teams may camp anywhere on the moor (minimum of 1km away from any checkpoints).

Teams must arrive back by 17:00 on the Sunday, having visited all ten tors on their route in order, to qualify for a medal and complimentary pasty. Teams that finish the challenge as a complete six also receive a certificate.

For all the competitors, there are tricky obstacles to overcome: the granite underfoot and the bogs, which lie in the valleys and dips, can catch you unawares. In addition, the weather on the North Moor can be treacherous and turn from warm and sunny to torrential rain and cold, literally in minutes. If you do not plan and prepare thoroughly, the Ten Tors Challenge in Dartmoor's unforgiving surroundings will catch you out.

Just before the summer school break in 1975, one of our teachers asked us to think about whether we wanted to take part in the 1976 Ten Tors Challenge and let him know on our return to school in September. I decided to go for it, along with a number of other schoolmates in my year group.

On our return after the school break, 12 of us, out of a year group of 90, had put our names forward and were allocated to one of the two teams that would be entered for the 35-mile challenge.

This is when our planning began.

At our first briefing with our new team members, we were advised of our Team Purpose: "To complete the 35-mile route, as a team of no less than four people, within the allocated time".

We were then each given a list of essential personal equipment that we needed to buy. Hiking boots, gaiters (waterproof leggings that clip onto hiking boots and go up to just under your knee), waterproof leggings and jacket, rucksack, sleeping bag, woollen socks, gloves, hat, water bottle, cutlery, cup, plate and compass.

There were then some shared items that needed to be purchased, such as two three-man tents, cooking stove, safety rope and first aid kit.

It was agreed that we would train every other weekend, so we had approximately 8 months, so 16 training walks. We started off by undertaking small walks of ten miles in one day on the South Moor, which had easier terrain.

As we did, it became apparent that we had different skills, which we naturally fell into. The leader, the motivator, the orienteer, the lookout, the cook and the first aider. Each different, however each incredibly important to the success of our team.

Every time we went out on a training walk, our trust in each other grew, as we helped each other when someone was finding the going tough, had blistered feet, or had fallen waist-high in a hidden bog.

As we grew in confidence, we upped the mileage until where we felt comfortable, walking 20 miles in a day. We then planned to sleep out overnight and increase the mileage. The winter months gave us the experience of walking in cold torrential rain all day, and on occasion hiking through snow. When the weather became finer in the spring, we also had the experience of walking in full hiking gear with heavy rucksacks in the heat of the day, which again had its challenges, one of which was dehydration.

When we camped for the night, we often had chats about what it would feel like as we passed the finishing line and succeeded. Little did I realise at the time that what we were doing was visioning, a technique that is a great motivator and often used by sportsmen and women.

We also discussed what was working well and what was not going so well that we needed to change.

Near the end of our training, we began to plan and then practise for different eventualities. What would we do if one of us became ill? Who would take over their duties? We were in effect contingency planning to mitigate potential risks.

On the Friday evening, we made our way to Okehampton Army Camp, on the eve of the Ten Tors Challenge. We watched the safety briefing film, had our essential equipment checked and were given the green light to start on the Saturday morning.

That evening we were allocated a space to pitch our two tents next to a team from London, who were undertaking the 35-mile route, as we were. We got into conversation with them and asked them how much training and planning they had done. We were astounded by the reply we received. "We've done a few laps around Hyde Park, carrying our rucksacks."

The next morning, we lined up with 400 other teams, at about 06:30, at which point we were given an envelope in which was our designated 35-mile route and the ten tors that we had to check into.

At 07:00, the cannon fired and 2,400 individuals, in 400 teams, set off in different directions across the rugged terrain of Dartmoor.

We reached our first checkpoint in good spirits and in good time. Our designated leader had our team sheet stamped to verify our check-in and then we were heading off to our next tor.

At our third check-in, we came across the team from London, who had camped next to us on the Friday night. Although we were both doing 35 miles, our routes were different, and for them this was their second check-in. As our leader went to get our team sheet stamped for the third time, the rest of us went over to chat with the other team.

It was then that we saw a paramedic with them. When we got closer, we realised that they had their socks and boots off and the paramedic was tending to their feet, which were already extremely blistered. In addition, one of their team had fallen over and sprained their ankle.

After a brief chat with the officials, it was agreed that they would take no further part in the competition, due to the ankle injury of one of their team and the blistered feet of the rest of them, so early on in the challenge.

It was then that it hit home to us how our planning and preparation was paying off.

A good day's hiking ensued, with the miles and the first day allowance of seven tors checked into achieved. Tents up and food eaten, we slept peacefully and soundly. Breakfast eaten, tents packed away and we were ready for the off at 06:00 on the Sunday morning, to complete the remaining three tors.

We eventually crossed the finishing line at midday on the Sunday, to be greeted by jubilant cheers and waves from family and friends who had made the journey to congratulate us.

A bronze medal for each of us, representing the 35-mile route we had accomplished, and a certificate for the whole team's achievement were gratefully accepted. Photographs taken by proud parents ensued and the most enjoyable part of the adventure followed, the complimentary pasty.

Buoyed by our success, we decided soon after to enter the 45-mile challenge the following year, which we did and succeeded in achieving. Unfortunately, none of our team completed the 55-mile challenge, as we were too focussed on studying for our exams when we were old enough for us to enter this one.

There was so much that, on reflection, I learned in terms of teamwork and importantly, the need for and importance of planning and preparing well, to reduce risks and increase the likelihood of success.

THE SUGGESTION

Whether you are part of a leadership, operational or project team, it is important that you get as many of your team as possible involved in the planning process. In doing so, you create ownership. As individuals, we have more affinity with and desire to achieve something that we have been part of creating.

Now the first thing to do with your team is to communicate the goal or target that has been set for you. Quite often, this will be set by someone external to the team. Hopefully, you have mutually agreed a goal that, whilst stretching, importantly is achievable.

At this moment in time, it is a good idea to review this goal, to ensure that it aligns with your Team Purpose. If it does not, due to changes of direction or strategy of your organisation, it is worthwhile spending time with your team on redefining your Team Purpose, to ensure that it is, pardon the pun, "fit for purpose".

Now depending on what type of team you work in, your goal or goals will be different.

An Operational team may have goals relating to effectiveness or efficiency of process, measured by error rates, downtime, deadlines hit.

A Project team may have goals relating to quality, budget or timescales.

An HR team may have goals relating to attrition rates, learning interventions and employee satisfaction.

These are just a few examples, and I'm sure that whatever team you lead, you will know what your goals are. The key to success is that these goals are SMARTA – Specific, Measurable, Achievable, Relevant, Timebound and most importantly Agreed.

BEPART of Planning Model

Once you know what your goals are and have checked out that your Team Purpose aligns with them, then you can begin to create your plans that will hopefully help you to achieve those goals.

One of the models that I have created, which has worked with many a team that I have used it with, is one I call BEPART. BEPART stands for the following:

Behaviours, **E**nablers, **P**reventers, **A**ctions, **R**esponsibilities, **T**imescales.

BEPART of Planning

Behaviours look to the future.

The Enablers and Preventers are present orientated.

Actions, Responsibilities and Timescales help map out and plan what is needed to get you from the present to the future.

The resources needed are six flipcharts or flipchart pages, one headed up for each constituent part of the **BEPART** Planning Model. In addition, a pad of Post-it notes and a pen for each team member.

The flipchart for the Behaviours should be divided into four quadrants. The quadrants should be headed up with the words Doing, Saying, Feeling and Thinking.

The flipchart for Preventers should be divided halfway horizontally and each half headed up Internal and External.

Here is how you work through each part with your team.

Behaviours
Get your team to imagine that they are in the future and have succeeded and achieved the team goals that have been set.

Get them to write down on a Post-it note what people will be Doing, Saying, Feeling and Thinking about the team, with one comment on each. Then get them to stick their comments in the appropriate quadrant.

Now, if you have read the chapter about colourful behaviours earlier in this book, you may have picked up that Doing is linked to the Red behavioural preference, Saying – Yellow, Feeling – Green and Thinking – Blue.

Based on the behavioural preferences of your team members, they will find writing comments about some quadrants easier than others, however we have all four within us, so it is important that they capture one comment for each of the four from each team member.

Once everyone has completed and stuck their comments onto the appropriate quadrants, it is useful to go through these with the team, to see whether there are similarities or differences in team members' comments.

This part of the process is often referred to as "visioning" and, as briefly mentioned earlier, is often used by sportsmen and women to get them into a positive frame of mind before their event, by imagining that they are actually doing it and are successful.

Enablers

Enablers are resources, skills, systems or technology that the team already has in place, that will help them achieve the goals set. Again, ensure that you get feedback, thoughts and ideas from all of the team, to capture the broadest amount of information.

Preventers

Preventers are things that will stop or block the team from succeeding. Again, it could be a person, a system or a process. When team members capture their thoughts, remember to stick them to the relevant part of the flipchart, either Internal or External.

Internal are things that can be changed from within the team, as opposed to External, which the team has no direct influence over. For example, this could be a system that is company-wide, that may not be fit for purpose. This will help to inform Actions that need to be taken, as to whether these occur within or external to the team.

Actions

Based on the work completed so far by your team, referencing the goals set and Team Purpose, the next stage enables the team to capture actions that need to be taken.

Responsibilities

Go through each Action captured and discuss it with the team. Will it help achieve the goals set? Is it practical? If there is a cost associated with the Action, are there funds that can be used?

Once the Action has been validated and agreed to be one that needs to be progressed, assign it to the most appropriate member to take it forward, as an Action. Whilst they are noted as being Responsible for the Action happening, it does not necessarily mean that they need to do it themselves, as they can also involve others with the relevant skills and knowledge to support them.

Timescales

Now, once all the Actions have been agreed, and Responsibilities assigned for each, this is where the Post-it notes come into their own.

Now, say for instance that you are putting together a yearly plan, the **Timescales** flipchart would be divided into 12 months.

You can then begin to go through the **Actions** and discuss the order of each. Does the Action come at the start of the 12 months or later? What is the first action that needs to be taken and by when?

The Post-it notes mean that, as you and your team go through this process, the timeline of actions can be changed easily, if it is found that one action is reliant on the completion of another, or whether certain actions can be run in parallel.

By the end of the **BEPART** of Planning session above, you should have a good outline of a plan that will help you and your team achieve the goals that you have been set.

Once your plan has been created and shared with your team, the final and really important thing to do is to set aside regular dates to review it with your team and update it, to ensure it continues to be a living, working plan.

In the interim, to keep the plan alive in the minds of your team, use visuals to keep it firmly in their minds. Consider a traffic light approach to visually represent what is not working, what is faltering and what is going well.

FOOD FOR THOUGHT

Q1. How often, once your plan is created, do you and your team review it?

Q2. How many of the team get involved in creating your plan?

Q3. Is your plan updated when changes occur?

Q4. Are the goals of individuals in your team linked to your team's plan?

LEARNING THROUGH LAUGHTER

Imagine the scene. You are seated with approximately 100 other leaders. The second speaker of the conference is 10 minutes into their 45-minute presentation. They are talking about the importance of planning in reducing risks and helping you and your team achieve your goals.

The conference is in a hotel in Battersea, next to the London Heliport, on the south bank of the River Thames.

You glance out of the window and see a pilot and co-pilot enter a black, sleek helicopter. They are followed by a man wearing a hi-vis jacket, beckoning a man and woman, both dressed in dark business suits and wearing sunglasses, towards the passenger seats in the back of the helicopter.

The man wearing the hi-vis jacket checks both of the passengers' safety harnesses, shuts the door, then proceeds to the front of the helicopter and gives the thumbs-up to the pilot and co-pilot.

The rotor blades begin to slowly turn. As they pick up speed, the noise of the rotors turning, which by now are a blur, gets louder and louder, filling the conference room.

You notice that the speaker's lips are moving, and the presentation slides are changing on the screen.

The helicopter rises into the air; noise still fills the room. It banks left and begins to disappear, the noise slowly fading as it gets further away.

As the noise level reduces to normal, you hear the presenter say, "Thank you for your time, it's been an absolute pleasure presenting to you, do you have any questions?"

You look at the person next to you, who has a similarly quizzical look on their face as you. You look at others around the room and see smiles breaking out on people's faces and laughter beginning to fill the air, as everyone realises that the presenter is joking.

The above story is true. The presenter was me and I did carry on and finish my presentation.

The learning is to always have a Plan B in whatever you are doing, as things, on occasion, do go wrong and it is those who are prepared for such situations that invariably overcome them.

The other learning is that if you are ever asked to speak at a conference, check out where the nearest heliport is!

PING MOMENTS

Time to reflect on this chapter and capture
any ideas that it has given you.

_____

_____

_____

_____

_____

_____

_____

_____

_____

_____

_____

_____

_____

_____

_____

CHAPTER 8

COLLABORATION:
ELEMENT 4 OF 16

*"A team is not a team, unless we all **Collaborate**,*
Sharing skills and knowledge that we have learnt to date.
For our efforts must be as one, if we are to succeed,
All for one and one for all, a behaviour we must breed."

Category: Creative Interactions

Team DyNAmics Definition: A joint effort between individuals, whereby the skills and knowledge of more than one person is required to achieve a common goal.

Etymology: From Latin, meaning work with.

Newbie: Why should I share the things that I have learnt with others?
Jules: So that your colleagues receive the gift of learning from you and can reciprocate, by giving you the gift of learning from them.

WHAT IS COLLABORATION?

*"Sharing our knowledge, experience, ideas and
skills with others results in the unachievable
for one being achieved by the many."*

Collaboration means different things to different people, however my definition, relating to teamwork, is two or more team members sharing their knowledge, their experience, their skills, ideas and thoughts, to achieve day-to-day tasks effectively, create something new or change something that already exists.

In a team, if things are not working well then you change them to make them better and on occasion changes that are imposed from outside of the team may require changes to be made to how the team works, which require both innovation and collaboration.

Collaboration between team members stacks the odds of success in favour of the team, with each individual becoming a valuable resource for the team.

Ideas are plentiful, based on a combination of the knowledge and also experience of individuals within the team and more effective decisions can be made, due to the diversity of behavioural decision-making preferences (see Thinking and Feeling in Chapter 2 of this book).

In addition, risks can be significantly reduced when based on a broader collective base of experience and knowledge.

BENEFITS

1. It saves time, increases productivity and helps **Transformation**.
2. It helps build **Trust** between team members.
3. **Planning** becomes more effective, due to knowledge sharing and experience.

4. It helps to promote a positive working **Environment**, by valuing and appreciating diversity of skills, knowledge, experience and behavioural styles.

RED FLAGS

1. Individuals are reticent to share their knowledge, skills and experience with others, preferring to see these as a competitive advantage that will benefit themselves.
2. Changes to working practices are frequently implemented by individuals, without consulting with others in the team.
3. Changes that are implemented regularly go wrong.
4. A "my way is the best and only way" culture exists.

THE STORY
Collaboration for the community

I had been working with a company of about 60 staff for a number of years, undertaking various learning and development interventions with them.

They had each had their individual behavioural profiles. They had undertaken 360-degree feedback, had coaching sessions, been part of team development sessions at leadership, operational and project team levels, explored trust, communication, stress management and much more; in fact there was not much left in my training kit bag.

Individuals, teams and the company had all benefited and there was very little else that could be delivered in terms of learning and development, however they wanted to explore whether there was any way in which the learning they had experienced could be put to good use, to give something back to their local community.

So I shared an idea that had worked exceptionally well for me in the past and had resulted in my team, whilst working for Barclays, winning a national "Make A Difference" award.

The concept was a simple yet powerful one that would utilise all the training that they had experienced and importantly, through effective collaboration, deliver a legacy to their community. The leadership team decided to accept my suggestion.

The initial stage was to communicate with the whole company the idea of undertaking one day's community work for a deserving cause of their choice. Staff were asked to nominate a cause that they thought was worthy.

Staff were also asked, at the time of making their choice, to provide a brief overview of the organisation that they had nominated.

Once all the nominations were in, a list was compiled that included brief overviews. This was then shared with everyone, with each person being given an opportunity to vote for their preferred three.

A shortlist of three was then compiled, based on the votes. On a specified day, the three shortlisted organisations came to the company's HQ and undertook a half-hour presentation to all the staff, which shared more about the organisation and the specific project they had in mind that needed to be completed.

The three shortlisted were:

1. A community hall that required redecoration and refurbishment, inside and out.
2. A wildlife trust that needed invasive shrubs removed from six sites across the county.
3. A spinal injury respite and rehabilitation centre that required a greenhouse erected and paths widened to allow wheelchair access.

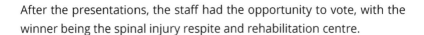

After the presentations, the staff had the opportunity to vote, with the winner being the spinal injury respite and rehabilitation centre.

The icing on the cake was that although there was one project chosen for the whole of the company to work with on a specified day, some staff felt so strongly about the two other projects that, of their own free will and in their own time, they volunteered to help them.

This is when a truly remarkable piece of collaboration kicked in, with the learning and development about behaviours, leadership and teamwork all being put to best use.

A Project Purpose Statement was created, so everyone had a common understanding of what they would be doing, what this would enable and the benefits. This brought the whole company together and had a positive impact on the already high levels of trust between individuals.

Teams were formed that played to people's strengths both from their behavioural skills and technical skills. Leaders were agreed.

One team was tasked with getting the required materials for the day, by begging or borrowing, so as to keep costs down to a minimum. They used their creativity to get local builder's merchants to offer materials in return for a mention in PR that they had planned.

Another team covered health and safety and logistics, ensuring staff would have transportation both to and from the centre and that insurance was in place to cover the manual work being undertaken. For the manual workers, appropriate safety gear was commissioned, again mostly free, in return for PR.

One team was in charge of the packed lunches and the celebration BBQ that it was agreed would be put on at the end of the day for staff and people using the centre, all the staff of the company, their families and those who had provided materials gratis.

This team was able to requisition a couple of huge marquees from the local army unit, cooking facilities, benches, tables and cutlery. Another member of this team managed to get a local wholesale food supplier to provide the food, at cost!

On the day, the weather was fine and spirits were high. Overgrown bushes were cut back, pathways widened, paving slabs laid, and a huge greenhouse erected. After starting at 8 am and working hard throughout the day, by 6 pm the project and work had been delivered.

The champagne corks popped and the smell of barbecued food soon pervaded the warmth of the evening air.

Much laughter and joy continued throughout the evening, with the resulting photographs, that subsequently appeared in the local paper, capturing this to great effect.

I hope you will agree, an incredible example of the positive impact that collaboration can have. I am glad to say that the positive impact, both for the organisation and community, lived on for many years afterwards.

THE SUGGESTION

The Gifts That I Bring to the Team

It is important that other team members know the skills, knowledge and experience of their colleagues and how these can support the team in achieving their goals.

Allocate 20 minutes as part of your team meetings to enable individuals to share this information.

Get a volunteer from the team to put together a presentation, lasting no more than 20 minutes. Give them a jointly agreed timescale to complete this, prior to the team meeting. They can choose to present in whatever way they wish i.e. free format or using presentation slides.

Their presentation should be no more than 15 minutes and include an overview of:

1. What their responsibilities are
2. Their past experience and how it helps currently
3. The technical skills that they utilise to complete their responsibilities
4. The behavioural skills that they use
5. Who they hand over from and to, as part of any team processes
6. Any challenges/risks that they are aware of
7. How they may be able to help others

At the end of their presentation, allow five minutes for any questions from other team members to clarify anything presented.

The above activity has two benefits. It supports the team in understanding more about the value that individual team members bring to the team, which will support collaboration. In addition, it helps the individuals to practise their communication and presentation skills.

You may also want to consider doing something similar when a member of your team attends a course. Provide them with an opportunity to share their experience with the rest of the team and how they will apply the learning to help the team achieve its goals.

FOOD FOR THOUGHT

Q1. How regularly do you experience collaboration between team members?

Q2. Do your subject matter experts freely share their expertise with the rest of the team?

Q3. When individuals complete learning, do they share what they have done and how it may help the team?

Q4. When an issue arises, is there lots of discussion by the team to help implement the best solution?

PING MOMENTS

Time to reflect on this chapter and capture
any ideas that it has given you.

_____

_____

_____

_____

_____

_____

_____

_____

_____

_____

_____

_____

_____

_____

CHAPTER 9:

ACCOUNTABILITY:
ELEMENT 5 OF 16

*"We each must be **Accountable**, right from the very start,*
To deliver quality in our team plan, relating to our part.
Then ensure a smooth handover, to our colleague who is next,
So we can, as a team, create a chain of excellence."

Category: Strategic Action

Team DyNAmics Definition: Individuals taking personal
responsibility for their actions and behaviours.

Etymology: From Old French, meaning state of being answerable.

Newbie: Isn't it a sign of weakness to own up
to the team about your mistakes?
Jules: It is possibly one of the strongest things that you can do.

WHAT IS ACCOUNTABILITY?

"In good teams, leaders hold individuals accountable. In great teams, everyone holds each other accountable."

Accountability is the commitment by an individual, if required, to explain their activities, accept responsibility for them and share the results they achieve, whether positive or negative, in a transparent and open manner with the rest of the team.

Ultimately, individual accountability is about ownership of the tasks and processes that you are responsible for delivering in the team.

To be accountable, each team member needs to understand what they need to do, when it needs to be completed and if appropriate to whom they hand over their part of the process next. In addition, they need to be empowered to own their part of any process.

Teams that have a high degree of individual accountability have team members that are comfortable being held accountable by their colleagues. The team creates an environment where individuals feel able to hold their hand up to any mistakes that are made, as they know that the team will support them to overcome these mistakes and learn from the experience.

The key to achieving a high degree of accountability within your team is:

1. Each individual having clarity about what the goals of your team are.
2. Having an understanding of how their individual responsibilities fit with team goals.
3. Appreciating that accountability is a positive element of teamwork.
4. Being aware that they will not be chastised when they make mistakes.

BENEFITS

1. Problems are identified quickly, as individuals will readily share problems with the team through effective **Communication**.
2. High standards are expected from all team members by all team members, helping to develop a positive **Environment**.
3. Decisions on what to do in a crisis or when something goes wrong are made easily with buy-in from all of the team, helping to achieve timely **Transformation**.
4. Support is readily given to team members, which helps to increase levels of **Trust**.

RED FLAGS

1. When mistakes are made, individuals pass the blame onto others.
2. Poor performance is accepted by the team and leader.
3. Individuals are blamed as opposed to supported when mistakes are made.
4. Individuals are rewarded for their efforts rather than the team being rewarded.

THE STORY
Too many bodies

Do you have Somebody, Nobody, Anybody or Everybody in your team?

The poem below is by an anonymous British poet.

> *This is a little story about four people named*
> *Everybody, Somebody, Anybody and Nobody.*
> *There was an important job to be done and*
> *Everybody was sure that Somebody would do it.*
> *Anybody could have done it, but Nobody did it.*
> *Somebody got angry about that because*
> *it was Everybody's job.*

Everybody thought that Anybody could do it, but
Nobody realised that Everybody wouldn't do it.
It ended up that Everybody blamed Somebody when
Nobody did what Anybody could have done.

I think this is a wonderful summary of lack of Accountability that can occur within teams.

As teamwork involves each team member playing their part in achieving the goals of the team, it is often akin to a relay race, with each person having their own part to play and having to ensure that their part of the process is handed on to the next member of the team in a way that enables a smooth and flawless transition to the next person, so they can complete their part of the process.

Failure at any part of the process will result in the team failing to meet its objective.

In a team with high levels of accountability, you will find that individuals will happily put up their hand and be held accountable by their colleagues, if a problem occurs. The team will review what went wrong, learn from the mistake and put in place new procedures and test them, to ensure that things run smoothly in the future.

In a team where there is lack of accountability, you will get the blame culture occurring, back-stabbing and finger-pointing (and we must always remember that one finger pointed at another means there are three pointing back at us!).

In my opinion, a great example of accountability is by the Formula One teams, when their driver makes a pit stop. The driver, car and pit team make up what is called the F1 Trinity. With the limited ability to overtake, combined with the small differences between the drivers and their cars' performance, the necessity for the individuals in the pit team to do their jobs effectively can mean the difference between winning, being on the podium or just ending up as an also-ran.

Everyone in the F1 Trinity knows exactly what they need to do, when they need to do it, who they hand over their part of the process to, and the overall goal of the team.

When mistakes are made, these are analysed and learnt from, with changes being implemented that are agreed by all and wherever possible tested, prior to the next race.

THE SUGGESTION

An activity that works well, that I have used many times with teams is called "Bridging the Gap".

The resources that you need are three flipcharts. If you are able, secure these to a wall.

Next, get the team to think about a particular piece of work that involved all or a large majority of them, that worked really well, was a success and demonstrated both individual and team accountability. Once they have agreed on one, capture the responses on the left-hand flipchart, based on the following:

- Overview of the piece of work that went well
- What made it work so well?
- How did it make you feel being part of the success?
- Were there any difficulties and if so, how were they overcome?

Once you have captured the above, get them to go through the same process, however this time get them to discuss a process that went really badly and demonstrated lack of individual and team accountability. Capture these on the right-hand flipchart.

- Overview of the piece of work that went badly
- What made it go wrong?
- How did it make you feel being part of this failure?
- What happened when difficulties occurred?

There should be a stark contrast in the information captured between the left and right-hand flipchart.

Finally, on the flipchart in the middle, get the team to discuss what needs to happen to make sure that moving forward there is both individual and collective accountability in everything that the team does.

What the team will have created is an Accountability Agreement and because they have all had input into creating it, they should all buy into it and uphold it in the future.

FOOD FOR THOUGHT

Q1. Do you know who owns each part of a process?

Q2. Have you created an end-to-end process map with personal accountability for each part of the process?

Q3. Do you hold each other accountable, in a positive and supportive way?

Q4. How does your team behave if something goes wrong?

PING MOMENTS

Time to reflect on this chapter and capture
any ideas that it has given you.

_____

_____

_____

_____

_____

_____

_____

_____

_____

_____

_____

_____

_____

_____

_____

_____

CHAPTER 10:

COMMITMENT:
ELEMENT 6 OF 16

"Sometimes things will be easy, sometimes they will be tough,
But if we all go above and beyond, it
should hopefully be enough,
*By showing our **Commitment**, we surely will pull through,*
And demonstrate to others what our team can really do."

Category: Coactive Connections

Team DyNAmics Definition: The energy, effort and time that individuals are prepared to invest in the team for it to achieve success.

Etymology: From Latin "committere", to unite, connect, combine, to bring together.

Newbie: When is the best time to show commitment to the team?
Jules: All of the time.

WHAT IS COMMITMENT?

"Commitment goes above and beyond a
promise, which is often too easily broken."

Commitment is that element of teamwork which you instinctively know whether your team has, or if it is lacking. Whilst it is important to have commitment when things are going well, it manifests and demonstrates itself most or not at all, when things have gone wrong.

It is the level of enthusiasm and responsibility that individuals have towards achieving team goals. Levels of commitment can often be understood based on how much pride individual team members have in their team, when they talk about it to others outside of the team.

When things have gone wrong, teams that have a high degree of commitment will roll their sleeves up and put in significant effort to put things right. As the title of the Billy Ocean hit single states, "When the going gets tough, the tough get going."

Probably one of the most powerful real-life stories about commitment is the Apollo 13 mission. The spacecraft launched from the Kennedy Space Center on April 11th 1970 and was meant to be the third mission to land on the moon.

The mission was aborted two days in, when an oxygen tank on the service module exploded and damaged vital parts of the spacecraft, not only ending the planned mission, but also putting the lives of the three astronauts, Jim Lovell, Jack Swigert and Fred Haise, in jeopardy.

The team at Mission Control in Houston had to generate ideas, then test out these ideas, as best they could in a limited period of time, to find a solution to save the astronauts based on the significant amount of damage to their spacecraft.

If you have not watched the movie *Apollo 13*, released in 1995 and starring Tom Hanks, I would highly recommend that you do, as you will better understand what high levels of commitment can achieve.

High levels of commitment are achieved in teams when individuals believe in what the team is trying to achieve, i.e. the team purpose, how what they deliver in their role makes a positive contribution to the overall success of the team, that their contribution is valued and appreciated by the rest of the team, and colleagues trust each other.

Finally, another thing that teams with high levels of commitment do is that they have fun, at appropriate times. As the saying goes, "All work and no play, makes Jack a dull boy."

BENEFITS

1. When things go wrong or an emergency arises, team members will devote energy and time **Collaborating** to find a solution.
2. Productivity is high, as individuals focus on delivering against their responsibilities in the **Role** they have in the team.
3. Milestones and deadlines are regularly achieved, due to effective **Processes** being in place.
4. Colleagues will help each other in times of difficulty, further enhancing **Trust**.

RED FLAGS

1. Destructive conversations occur about the purpose of the team and therefore priorities.
2. Excessive analysis of situations to try to find flaws occurs.
3. Frequent talk about "It's just a job" or "Well, it pays the bills".
4. Demonstration of a lack of urgency or willingness to put in additional effort or time when issues arise that need to be addressed in a timely fashion.

THE STORY
The missing finger

I had been asked to facilitate a three-hour learning session, with a directorate of 150 people who worked in approximately 15 teams. I had split the session into one and a half hours of learning and the remainder was set aside for the teams to apply the learning to practical real-life situations using activities, so the teams generated ideas and solutions to enhance their effectiveness.

At the midway coffee break, I was with a group of the team members when a guy joined the group. I noticed him out of the corner of my eye, because he was a couple of inches taller than my 6 foot 4 inches and considerably more muscular.

At an appropriate gap in the general conversation, he thanked me for my interactive and inspirational learning and additionally told me that he had also enjoyed my Janner sense of humour.

I found that interesting, as a Janner is a term associated with someone who was born in Plymouth, my city of birth.

My curiosity kicked in and I asked him how he knew the phrase. He replied that it was because he was born and brought up in Torpoint, which is the first town across the Tamar River when you cross into Cornwall via the Tamar Bridge.

He then continued by saying that he would have gone as far as giving me a high five for my session however was unable to do so.

With that, he proceeded to hold up his right hand, spreading his fingers, at which point I suddenly realised that his index finger was completely missing! A big smile spread across his face and he began to laugh, saying that he knew I wouldn't have expected that.

I laughed and enquired how he had lost his finger. He told me and the rest of the group around us that after school he had joined the Royal

Navy and a few years after joining, had been selected for the Devonport Field Gun Crew.

Now when I was a young lad, each year, at Earl's Court, London, the Royal Tournament was held. It was led in rotation by the Army, Navy and Royal Air Force, with a different theme each year. For a number of years, I made an annual trip from Plymouth to London with my mum, gran and auntie to watch it.

One of the highlights each year was the Field Gun Competition between Devonport, Portsmouth and the Fleet Air Arm Field Gun Crews.

At each performance of the Royal Tournament, two crews competed to transport a 12-pounder field gun and limber over a series of obstacles.

From the start line in front of the Royal Box, the crews pulled the guns and limbers to the end of the arena where they turned and carried themselves and the equipment over a five-foot wall. The guns and limbers were then dismantled and carried to the top of a ramp on the "home side" of a 28-foot chasm.

The crew set up a wire and traveller so all 18 members of the crew and their equipment could cross the chasm. The team and equipment then passed through a hole in the "enemy wall" at the end of the arena. Each crew then fired three rounds to end the "run out".

The second part of the competition (the "run back") involved the crews taking all their equipment back over the five-foot (1.5m) enemy wall and then back across the chasm. Once all the crew and equipment were back on the home side of the chasm, the wire and traveller were dismantled and three more rounds were fired in a rearguard action.

In the final stage, the "run home", men, guns and limbers passed back through the hole in the home wall and then the teams "hook up and pull for home". The clock was stopped as the teams crossed back over the start line.

The guy who had lost his index finger was in charge of one of the wheels on the gun carriage. To get it across the chasm, the linchpin that held the wheel onto the wheel shaft had to be removed and the wheel put onto his shoulder, before he swung across the chasm on the zipwire. On the other side, the wheel would be reassembled onto the wheel shaft, together with the rest of the gun, which was hauled to the finish line by all the crew.

Now, when he was on the "run back", he had dropped the linchpin. He placed the wheel onto the wheel shaft and had to make a split-second decision on how to keep the wheel on there for the run home. You've probably guessed by now that he decided to keep it on by putting his finger where the linchpin should go.

He then told us that when the gun went to start the "run home", with one revolution of the wheel his finger had been chopped off; however, he added with a big grin, "we won the race".

Now, in terms of individual commitment to the team, personally I do not think I have heard anything that can beat that.

There is some incredible archive footage if you search on YouTube for Field Gun Crew, as the Royal Tournament ended in 1999.

THE SUGGESTION

An activity that clarifies commitment, always works extremely well and is also very positive is something that I call "WE Commit".

Notice the block capitals of the word WE, as everyone in the team needs to sign up to the output.

Stage 1 is to split your team into groups of no more than four people per group. If you have a team that has less than six people in it, no problem, just work as one team.

The idea is for each group to discuss and agree as many things as possible that they think, as individuals and as a team, they can commit to do.

If you want, you can share some examples, such as:

- We commit to welcoming new members to our team positively.
- We commit to helping colleagues who are under pressure or have encountered a problem.
- We commit to talking positively about our team to others.

Hopefully, based on the above, you will get the idea.

Next, give the groups some paper and a pen to capture their ideas. Agree a spokesperson for each group and give the groups a time limit of say 15 minutes.

When the time is up, allow each group to share their commitments, capturing them on a flipchart. If one group has a similar or the same commitment as another group on the flipchart, just annotate x2 or x3 beside it.

Once all the groups have finished sharing, you will have a list of commitments. Number these commitments up. So you may have 1 to 15, for example.

Next, give each member of the team a piece of paper. Get them to read the commitments on the flipchart and write down on their piece of paper the numbers of any commitments that they feel they cannot sign up to.

Gather the pieces of paper in and for any numbers they have written down, mark an X against the corresponding commitment on the flipchart.

Whilst you could do this part of the activity as an open forum discussion, with people verbally letting you know which they cannot commit to, some people feel more comfortable with the anonymity. You know your team better than me as to what would work best for you.

Hopefully, after you have crossed through the ones with an X beside them, you should end up with what I call a "Contract of Commitments".

Based on my experience, I would suggest that you need between 5–10 commitments. If you have less than 5, you may want to open up a discussion to generate a few more. In my experience, unless you have a real issue within the team relating to commitment, you should get between 5–10 easily, and often many more.

If you get more than 10, say 13, then get individuals to mark on the flipchart the 3 they like the least. You should then be able to narrow it down to 10.

The final part is to get the Contract of Commitments typed up and get everyone in the team to sign it, to demonstrate that they helped create it and are committed to demonstrating them.

Perhaps every six months, have a team session where you review what you had drawn up. Is it working? Are any changes needed?

Oh, and one last thing, make sure new members to the team are made aware of this Contract of Commitments, as part of their induction process.

FOOD FOR THOUGHT

Q1. Do you see team members' commitment demonstrated regularly?

Q2. What happens when a colleague has a problem?

Q3. Do team members watch the clock for going home time or do they finish the task they are doing?

Q4. In meetings or conversations, how frequently do you hear, "That's not my problem" or "It's nothing to do with me"?

PING MOMENTS

Time to reflect on this chapter and capture
any ideas that it has given you.

_____

_____

_____

_____

_____

_____

_____

_____

_____

_____

_____

_____

_____

_____

_____

_____

CHAPTER 11:

ROLES & SKILLS:

*"**Roles and Skills** that complement, that is the winning feat,*
Like pieces of a jigsaw, they dovetail nice and neat.
Each member of our team, knowing what they and others do,
We all have our part to play, which will help to see us through."

Category: Framework Mapping

Team DyNAmics Definition: Understanding who is best suited
to undertake a task, both technically and behaviourally.

Etymology: Role, from Old French, meaning paper scroll, where an
actor's part was written, and skill, from Middle Dutch, meaning ability.

Newbie: How do you know when the right people
are in the right roles in the team?
Jules: You don't know it, you feel it.

WHAT ARE ROLES & SKILLS?

"When you have the right person, with the right
skills, in the right role, it just feels right."

In Chapter 2, I shared the importance of team members knowing each other's behavioural and technical skills, so I will not go into detail on this again, as you will have either read that chapter or have the option to go back and read it.

My focus here is therefore on the Roles aspect of this Element.

As we know, within a team there are many different roles that individuals undertake. You may have individuals whose focus is on the quality of output, others who may provide I.T. support. Others who keep track of the finances. Customer facing staff, who ensure that customers' needs are met, and in the majority of teams, a leader, who has overall accountability for the performance of the team. I have no doubt that you can think of many others in addition to those that I have mentioned.

The key is playing to the strengths of the people in your team, by ensuring that the people/technical skills of individuals complement the roles that they undertake. This is why, often, heterogeneous teams have an advantage over homogeneous teams.

When you get the right people in the right roles, it also has a significant positive impact on individuals, who will be motivated and inspired to give the best of themselves for the benefit of the team and in doing so, it also has a positive impact on the working environment and culture of the team.

A lot of teams, however, overlook this important aspect of teamwork and unfortunately individuals end up in roles that do not make best use of their people/technical skills, often resulting in mediocre performance and, indeed, just going through the motions.

When the above happens, it has a negative ripple effect, impacting on other team members and the performance of the team overall.

For any of you who play or watch team sport, just think about the teams that you watch. If they are good they will spend a considerable amount of time ensuring that the roles and skills of individuals are utilised to best effect.

Apart from the occasional unusual situation, you will not see a goalkeeper playing as a striker, nor indeed a striker playing in goal. It is all about getting the right people with the right skills in the right roles.

In addition, using the analogy of driving a car to a destination with passengers in it, you would not put someone who had not driven before in the driver's seat to drive you there.

BENEFITS

1. You are able to play to people's strengths, which has a positive impact on the working **Environment** of the team.
2. Team members recognise and appreciate what they and their colleagues bring to the team, thus valuing **Diversity**.
3. **Planning** is enhanced by utilising the skills of individuals effectively.
4. Knowledge sharing will occur more frequently as individuals increase their expertise in a particular role, thus positively impacting on **Collaboration**.

RED FLAGS

1. Individuals demonstrate frustration or appear bored with the job they do.
2. Being distracted onto other "more exciting things" happens frequently.
3. Productivity reduces and mistakes are made on a regular basis.

4. Tasks are undertaken that are not part of their remit or responsibility.

THE STORY
Right people, right roles, right result

After leaving Barclays and prior to setting up my first team development company, I undertook an interim role as a change management consultant, as I had undertaken this role whilst with Barclays.

My first appointment was to help support the rollout of a software upgrade to approximately 3,000 operational staff who worked in a 24/7 business. The rollout affected four different sites in the UK and was co-ordinated by the I.T. team, based at the main operational site.

I was aware that the I.T. team had a pretty poor reputation within the end user business community.

My first task was to find out from the end users why they had a poor perception of the team. So I asked the key contacts in the business areas and this is what they told me.

The technology rollouts work, however are rolled out at times that do not work for our operations.

Communication about rollouts is always via email and if a problem arises, we have to send an email to the help desk.

We are always speaking to different people, with nobody dedicated to our department and our needs.

They email us about rollouts, however use technical jargon that we do not really understand.

Based on the above, I could understand the frustration from the business user community.

At a meeting with the I.T. team, I shared a summary of the findings and they nodded their heads and agreed.

Now, it appeared to me that whilst the team had some incredible people and technical skills, they were not utilising these to best effect when undertaking the rollout of new software. The solution was to assign appropriate roles to team members as part of the rollout that maximised the use of both their people and technical skills. Having profiled them, I was aware of the different people strengths that they had, which proved beneficial.

During a team meeting, I shared the roles that I suggested were needed during the project:

- Project Communications
- Business Community Liaison
- Technical Support and Resolution
- Strategy and Planning

The team used their behavioural profiles to agree leads in each of these roles, with the remainder of the team providing support to the above, as required.

The Business Community Liaison had meetings with each business area, to understand the best times for them to implement the software upgrades, so as to mitigate the risk to their operational responsibilities and service to their customers.

This was fed back to the Strategy and Planning lead, who put together a timeline for rollout based on this, bearing in mind resources available to the team.

The Communication lead then created a Q&A business presentation for all the business areas in the lecture auditorium, talking them through what the upgrade meant in layman's terms, the timeline, what would happen during the upgrade and the on-floor support as soon as the upgrade had happened.

Concerns from the business areas were captured and solutions fed back, using a project bulletin.

During the six-month rollout, the Technical Support and Resolution sub-team were on hand at each different business area site to deal with any issues as soon as they arose.

During the rollout, out of the 3,000 upgrades, only 30 issues could not be resolved in the first hour, just 1% of the total.

It was a brilliant result for the team. They felt proud about what they had achieved, both as individuals and as a team, and their reputation within the business user community increased vastly.

After I left, I kept in touch with the team and was pleased to find out that they had continued to use the learning relating to aligning roles and skills on future rollout projects.

THE SUGGESTION

This is probably most appropriate for a team leader to undertake. I would suggest, as part of regular 1:1 performance reviews throughout the year, that time is set aside to not only discuss performance but also an individual's role.

The following questions should provide a good understanding of whether an individual is enjoying their role and if not, why not, so that hopefully something can be done about it.

Q1. On a scale of 1–10, how motivated are you in the role that you undertake?

Q2. What could be done to increase the score above?

Q3. What would need to happen to support you getting there?

Q4. What benefits to the team would occur if that happened?

The answers to the above should give a pretty good indication of whether an individual is motivated or not in the role that they are undertaking and whether anything can be done to increase their motivation. If nothing can be changed, then it may be an opportunity to consider a new role for that individual, either within the team or as part of another team.

FOOD FOR THOUGHT

Q1. Are the roles of team members discussed on a regular basis, as part of performance reviews throughout the year?

Q2. Is there frequent talk about individuals not liking their role or being bored?

Q3. Do individuals make the same mistakes on a regular basis?

Q4. Is the atmosphere within the team flat, as people just go through the motions?

PING MOMENTS

Time to reflect on this chapter and capture
any ideas that it has given you.

_____

_____

_____

_____

_____

_____

_____

_____

_____

_____

_____

_____

_____

CHAPTER 12:

COMMUNICATION: ELEMENT 8 OF 16

*"**Communication** that is effective, so
we know what's going on,
Should help us all ensure that nothing does go wrong.
So email, text or face to face, make sure our comms are good,
And whatever is the message, by all it's understood."*

Category: Creative Interactions

Etymology: From Latin, meaning to share.

Team DyNAmics Definition: The lifeblood of the team, enabling information to be shared, ideas generated and discussed, and decisions made.

Newbie: Why is effective communication in a team so important?
Jules: Because it is the foundation upon which collective clarity and understanding is built.

WHAT IS COMMUNICATION?

"Effective communication only occurs when the message sent is understood by ALL who receive it."

Communication is the way in which we impart or exchange information by speaking, writing or using another medium. Road signs are an example of visual communication.

In teams, it is one of the areas of teamwork that comes up time and time again as not working as effectively as it could for everyone.

Sometimes just hearing the chats about communication between the sender of the communication or the receiver of communication will give you clues that it is not working correctly.

Sender	Receiver
They just don't get it.	I've not got a clue what they are on about!
I might as well be talking to a brick wall. Why don't they reply?	Don't they realise I need time to consider what they've said?
What's wrong with graphs and images?	It's all very good sharing colourful graphs, however, where's the data?
I think the business benefits are totally clear.	What about the impact on people?

For those of you who have read Chapter 2 which included behavioural preferences, you may have already begun to realise that some of the above relate to when the sender and receiver have opposing preferences and, to put it simply, are not on the same wavelength.

I often say to teams that for communication between individuals within a team to be as effective as possible, you need to find the Goldilocks Zone, not too little, not too much, not too impersonal, not too personal, however just right. Believe you me, it is difficult to achieve, however not impossible.

Invariably, if your team is anything above five individuals, you are more than likely to have quite a mix of communication styles and preferences. These preferences can often be seen demonstrated in the emails that individuals send. Below are some examples that I have seen over the years.

Blue (Introverted Thinking)	Red (Extraverted Thinking)
1. A more formal approach with the focus on gathering or seeking information or providing it	Brief and to the point Focus on tasks and actions May not use your name
2. Often uses bullet point numbers and sub-indentation	May use CAPITALS for URGENCY or to EMPHASISE IMPORTANCE, or ACTION
3. Seeks information by stating, "I have a few questions" or "Would you provide me with further information"	"I need this by this date" "I want this completed immediately"
4. When providing information, will add attachments for additional clarification	

Green (Introverted Feeling)	Yellow (Extraverted Feeling)
Builds the relationship first before the task	More chatty/lengthy emails which may often leave you out of breath reading them!
Will regularly use your name at the start and within the email	May start with Hi, Hiya or How's it going?
Often starts with, "I hope this email finds you well"	Positive with ideas and thoughts
Will often tone down requests:	Why use one exclamation mark when you can use lots!!!!!!!
"I am sorry to bother you"	Often uses more emoticons ☺ ☺ ☺ to emphasise
"Would you mind"	
"When would it be convenient for you to..."	Watch out for "Wow", "Amazing", "Brilliant"

Whilst the above are extremes for each preference to emphasise the point, you may see some elements of your writing style in some of the examples above, or indeed the style of some of your colleagues.

So, bearing in mind that you are likely to have a mix of those with different communication needs and styles in your team, when communicating, whether it be face to face, via email, a formal document or presentation, the most effective way to hit the Goldilocks Zone is to use a mix of styles that will resonate with a greater breadth of individuals.

I have often used the phrase "Do unto others as **THEY** would be done unto" to get people thinking about this. As you will see this is a slight twist on the original phrase, "Do unto others as you would have done unto you", which dates back to around 500 BC.

What I am trying to get across to you is that if you communicate in your own style, the chances are that it may not be received and understood in the way you wanted it to be.

BENEFITS

1. Provides clarity and understanding, especially important to keep everyone focussed on the **Purpose** of your team.
2. **Decision-Making** becomes more effective, as everyone understands how the decision has been made.
3. It recognises the **Diversity** of team members' communication needs.
4. Enables **Processes** to be documented in a way that there is common understanding.

RED FLAGS

1. Lots of questions arise when a communication is sent to the whole team.
2. Processes go wrong, especially at the handover points between colleagues.
3. Individuals go off and do their own thing as they are not clear on priorities.
4. A lot of time is spent in meetings helping people to understand.

THE STORY
Connected communication

I had been working with a client for a short period of time, specifically with their leadership team, invited to do so by their director, Pam.

Pam and I had worked together previously at a number of organisations. Whenever Pam had moved on to a new challenge, invariably she would get in touch with me so I could work with her new colleagues and teams.

The facilitated sessions I had delivered, which focussed on their leadership styles, had obviously been well received, as Pam had invited me to deliver a keynote presentation at their annual conference, in front of the 200+ staff in the directorate.

I arrived in good time, about an hour and a half before the conference began, to check the room, ensure that my presentation slides loaded OK onto the conference room projection system and also check in with the AV team, to agree timings for me to be miked up before my session. The last thing I did, to get me into the zone, was a visualisation technique which had worked well for me when I had spoken at other conferences.

With that completed, I had time to have a coffee and chat with those staff who had begun to arrive, ready for the conference to begin at 9.

Pam's presentation focussed on sharing the planned changes over the next 12 months, and in doing so, set the scene for subsequent presenters and their presentations. As such, it was important that the messages she delivered landed effectively with the whole of the staff attending.

At 8.55, the tune and lyrics of "Changes" by David Bowie filled the conference room. Staff finished chatting to each other, finished drinking their teas/coffees and juices and made their way to their seats.

As the music faded, Pam appeared on stage. Once the chatter from the staff eventually faded, Pam began her presentation which, an hour later, I realised had been a masterclass in communication, using a lot of the techniques that I had shared with her over the years, which she had obviously found of value.

She started off by setting out the changes that had been planned, focussing on why the objectives and goals had been chosen and their benefits, both to the organisation and also to their clients and potential new clients.

Standing in one place, directing her eye contact to different staff in the audience, she used four fingers to count out the objectives and then used her hand to emphasise key points on her presentation slides.

She finished by highlighting the team members who would be the point of contact for each of the different workstreams. Her style was fast, direct and results focussed, supported by her delivery style and the brevity of information on the slides she used.

Pam moved seamlessly into another delivery style as she enthused about how the changes would provide exciting opportunities for individuals, teams and the organisation. Her body language became more animated as she moved to and fro across the stage, using her arms to visually demonstrate how these changes would involve everyone. Her presentation slides used more visuals and less words to bring the journey of the next 12 months to life, focussing on the many opportunities.

Pam then slowed things down, and with a warmth to her voice shared the fact that the changes mentioned would require everyone to develop, grow and learn new skills, if the goals were to be achieved. She reassured everyone that support would be provided, as would the appropriate training to ensure that everyone had the opportunity to upskill and meet the demands that the future held. She also shared that there would be small working groups set up to ensure any concerns could be voiced, listened to, and importantly responded to.

Finally, Pam explained the risks identified in delivering the 12-month plan, showing slides which included timelines, milestones, budgets, returns on investment and bonuses that would be available, provided the plan was delivered. She presented all of this in a calm manner, with very little inflection in her voice, as she stated the facts and figures. She also shared where more detailed information could be found, which would be regularly updated.

Pam completed her presentation almost exactly 45 minutes into her hour, providing 15 minutes for questions from the staff, which she covered effortlessly, making sure that any she was unable to answer immediately were noted and followed up after the conference.

After the next presenter, there was a coffee break, which enabled me to speak to a broad selection of staff. I simply asked what they thought of Pam's presentation. Each replied that they had found it extremely clear, beneficial and insightful, and that it was as though she was communicating with them individually.

What Pam had done was to recognise the different communication needs of her staff and use slides, words, tone of voice and body language that were congruent for each of the four high-level behavioural types I explained earlier in this book, which I hope that you may have spotted.

Pam had simply gone around the colours, in terms of her presentation, Red, Yellow, Green and Blue.

THE SUGGESTION

If you are not utilising profiling within your team, I would recommend that you consider it. Most highly-regarded profiling tools will include pages that, for individuals, will list Communication Do's and Don'ts.

If you don't use profiling, just ask team members to write down one thing in relation to communication that really works for them and one thing that doesn't work for them.

A communication do from my profile is "Allow Nick time to discuss a situation with others who are involved". This picks up on the fact that I like to listen to the thoughts, ideas and perspectives of others, so that when I make a decision, I can take these into account, and hopefully decide on the most effective action to take.

A do not from my profile is "Do not spend too much time on making points". I am one of those people who gets the gist of what is being said without needing the same point to be reiterated over and over again.

If everyone in the team writes down one do and one don't, you can then create a list which can be shared with everyone in the team. You could also take it a stage further and at your next team meeting, share them and get individuals to explain or expand on what they have written, to clarify for other team members.

Making Sure We Are AOK

Another activity that you can undertake within your team that enhances communication between individuals is something that I call "Making Sure We Are AOK". AOK stands for All OK and is attributed as being used by the astronaut Alan Shepard to let ground control know that all was OK.

This activity is completed on a 1:1 basis, by individuals in the team. Each team member should make sure that they complete it with each of their colleagues. This activity should be completed about once every quarter.

On a piece of paper, each individual writes down something that the other person does, in terms of their interactions and communication, that works well for them.

In addition, if there is anything that the other person does that does not work and needs to be discussed and changed, they also write this down.

When they have both got a convenient time to sit down and have a chat, perhaps over a coffee, they each share what they have written. By sharing the things that are working well, each of them receives positive confirmation and in essence a "thank you, please keep doing this, as it works for me".

If there is something that is not working, they discuss this, agree what needs to change and then they contract to make those changes.

Whilst some people may think that sharing something that isn't working in a relationship with another person could be quite difficult, it is in fact really positive and beneficial, because if things are left unsaid, they eventually will fester and cause a big problem in the relationship. Sometimes, the discussion goes beyond just communication, however is still beneficial, as you will read below.

I undertook the above activity as part of a team development session I was facilitating. I had previously been briefed that there were two people on the team who did not like each other at all.

When it came to this activity and it was their turn to pair off, I made sure to keep an eye on what was happening.

Within five minutes I heard laughter coming from both of them. I walked over and asked if all was OK.

"It is now," one of them replied.

The root cause of the demise of their relationship turned out to be the fact that when one of them asked the other to share their knowledge and experience, they would sit on the edge of the other team member's desk whilst waiting for a reply.

All the other was thinking in their head was "Get off my desk, you are in my space". However they had never told the other person so they kept doing it, because they didn't realise that in doing so they were upsetting the other.

A great example of what happens when something is not working and it is left to fester.

Finally, in terms of communication, when it is to more than one person, you should be thinking of including a mix of the below, to ensure that you maximise understanding and of course, hit the Goldilocks Zone of communication.

Blue (Introverted Thinking)	Red (Extraverted Thinking)
Provide information	Highlight business benefits
Put it in writing	Summarise key points
Share risks	Include timescales and milestones
Advise of where to find more detail	Provide points of contact details
Green (Introverted Feeling)	**Yellow (Extraverted Feeling)**
Include people benefits	Share positive future benefits
Demonstrate care & empathy	Use graphs/images/videos
Share how to give their feedback	Let them know how they can get involved
Provide details of where to get support	Include information on opportunities

FOOD FOR THOUGHT

Q1. Does everyone in the team know what works, in terms of each other's communication styles and needs?

Q2. What is the most common communication style in your team?

Q3. Are team communications too frequent, too infrequent or just right?

Q4. How long ago was the effectiveness of communication discussed by your team?

PING MOMENTS

Time to reflect on this chapter and capture
any ideas that it has given you.

_____

_____

_____

_____

_____

_____

_____

_____

_____

_____

_____

_____

_____

_____

_____

CHAPTER 13:

DECISION-MAKING: ELEMENT 9 OF 16

*"**Decisions** agreed, we must embrace with positivity,*
So we move forward as a team, using our ability.
If just one is out of sync, we'll get into a mess,
And sorting out the issue will cause us lots of stress."

Category: Strategic Action

Team DyNAmics Definition: Clarity about who has
the authority to make what decisions and when.

Etymology: From the Latin, meaning to cut off.

Newbie: What should you do if you cannot make a decision?
Jules: Explore whether a decision actually
needs to be made in the first place.

WHAT IS DECISION-MAKING?

*"The decision-makers of today are the
change-makers of tomorrow."*

Whether a decision is made by a team member or by the team collectively, the key to making the right decision is ensuring that an holistic approach has been taken in coming to the decision.

What do I mean by holistic? Well in Chapter 2, I provided an overview of two of the psychological preferences we have that impact on how we make decisions, given their names by Carl Jung as Thinking and Feeling. If you have not read it, or cannot remember what was said in that chapter, I would suggest that it would probably be beneficial for you to do so at this point.

As we have a preference for making decisions from either a Thinking or Feeling preference, we may overlook considering the decision from the opposing preference.

As an example, if you have a preference for Feeling, you may make a decision that meets the needs of as many people as possible, keeping them happy and your relationship with them positive, however you may overlook the achievement of the objectives that you have been tasked with.

Similarly, if you have a preference for Thinking, you may gather data and information upon which to make your decision but overlook the impact that your decision may have on people.

My preference is for making decisions from a Feeling preference, keeping relationships harmonious, however I learnt a lesson early on in one of my leadership roles that has stayed with me to this day.

Being young and naïve about leadership, at the time of performance reviews for my team I would have sleepless nights, especially if I knew that someone hadn't achieved the goals and targets that they had been set or had not behaved in a way that upheld our values and behaviours.

I would lie awake at night, thinking how that individual would hate me because I had made a decision and needed to tell them that they were not getting a bonus. I would imagine them telling their colleagues, friends and family and they would all hate me as well.

One of my peers saw me one day with an obviously troubled look on my face, and I shared the above with them.

They had a preference for Thinking and gave me some advice that helped me greatly. The advice was to simply have the data to hand to explain that they had not achieved the desired levels of achievement that warranted a bonus. In addition, they told me that writing it down on a piece of paper also depersonalised it as you would focus the discussion, referencing the piece of paper.

Finally, they said that you could use the Feeling preference to discuss how the individual could change things and the support available to help them to do so.

So simple, yet so effective, and using this idea enabled me to sleep peacefully thereafter at the time of performance reviews.

So the first part about decision-making in a team is ensuring that you have a holistic approach and look at a decision from both a Thinking and Feeling preference.

Secondly, any decisions made should be tested to ensure that they align to the team's purpose and support the achievement of set goals.

Thirdly, it is important that everyone in the team knows who has the appropriate authority to make decisions and also who has delegated authority, when the usual person who makes that decision is unavailable. This is something that is often overlooked and causes issues when someone is off work ill or on vacation.

Additionally, when it comes to group decisions, you need to have clarity about how the final decision is made.

Is it made by one individual, a few nominated individuals, the majority of the team or the whole of the team?

When it comes to group decisions, again it is important to understand the group preference. Is it Thinking or Feeling and is the lesser preference taken into account when deciding what decision to make?

BENEFITS

1. Ensures that any decisions made support the team's **Purpose** and goals.
2. Utilises the different decision-making **Skills** that individuals have.
3. Aids **Planning**, by ensuring decisions are based on a holistic view.
4. Enhances the effectiveness of decisions made at **Team Meetings**.

RED FLAGS

1. Individuals do not stick to decisions that have been agreed by the team.
2. Individuals overstep their decision-making authority.
3. It is difficult for decisions to be agreed by the team.
4. Individuals "pass the buck" to others to make a decision.

THE STORY
Should we stay or should we go?

I was facilitating some individual and team development with a team who looked after the I.T. systems for a large organisation. The team were first line support engineers and predominantly led with Green and Blue energies.

As usual, I had arrived at the hotel in good time to set up my equipment and ensure that the room layout was suitable for their team development. On arrival, the functions manager greeted me and began to lead me down the hotel corridor to the training room that had been allocated.

Whilst walking, she let me know that at the end of the previous week there had been an outbreak of norovirus, also called the winter vomiting bug. She told me that the hotel had been closed and that it had been deep cleaned. If however I was not happy, a training room was available at their sister hotel, about ten miles away.

I responded that, based on the deep clean, everything sounded fine, however I would check with the team that I was working with.

I set to, setting up my laptop, the projector and screen, turning everything on to make sure it all worked. I made a few adjustments to the layout of the room and ensured that the workshop materials and profiles were to hand.

Finally, I set up my portable speaker and began to play an upbeat playlist as the team arrived and enjoyed the jelly beans in bowls around the room, supplied by the hotel.

By 9.25 am, they had all arrived, ready for the 9.30 am start.

It was at this point that I shared the information that I had been given about what had happened over the weekend. Leading with Yellow energy, I felt sure that the team would be happy to stay at the hotel.

The team huddled together and began a discussion. I let them carry on and after about ten minutes, one of the team told me they had made a decision.

The group had decided that they could not risk one of their team falling ill and therefore wanted to move to the sister hotel. It was quite apparent that their dominance of Green energy had led them to make this decision, based on the wellbeing of their colleagues.

Fascinatingly, Blue, which was their secondary energy, kicked in as the spokesperson let me know that the main time spent discussing and agreeing a solution was not about the wellbeing of their colleagues but planning how best to travel to the other hotel.

They had checked who had transport and who had not. Who knew where the other hotel was? Who had satnav? What was the postcode of the other hotel? What was the most effective way to go in convoy, to ensure nobody got lost? Did they have mobile contacts, so they could keep in touch?

The above was a wonderful demonstration of group decision-making, where there is a particular dominance of behavioural preferences that impact on the decision-making process.

So I, leading with my Yellow energy, smiled, scooped up a few handfuls of jelly beans for the journey and began to pack up my equipment and resources to make the ten-mile drive to our new learning venue.

It was also a good learning point for me, with my Yellow energy preference, as I had forgotten the group preference of those I was working with!

THE SUGGESTION

My suggestion would be as follows:

1. Firstly, get each individual to go through each of their processes and note any decisions that have to be made by them, highlighting those that have greater risks attached to them if the wrong decision is made.
2. Then get them to consider who would be best suited to make a decision as to what needs to be done in their absence.
3. Capture the process to which the decision relates:
   a. At what point within the process the decision is made

b. Who the nominated decision-maker is when the primary decision-maker is absent.

3. Once individuals have documented their own, then it would be a good idea to amalgamate them and maybe have a session with the whole of the team, going through them so that everyone is aware of them and also to agree that they will step in when required, if they have been highlighted as the person to do so.

Secondly, in terms of team decisions, you may wish to consider creating a charter. The first thing to do would be to understand who prefers making decisions from a Thinking or Feeling preference and what the overall team preference is, based on an amalgamation of individual preferences.

In addition, you then need to decide, when you are making decisions as a team, are they made by one individual, a few nominated individuals, the majority of the team or the whole of the team?

Undertaking the above should provide you with a good foundation upon which effective decision-making can occur within your team.

FOOD FOR THOUGHT

Q1. Do individuals stick to decisions that are agreed by your team?

Q2. Are decisions that are made holistically thought through to get the best solution?

Q3. Do people shy away from making a decision or deferring it to someone else?

Q4. Do you know the key decisions that need to be made in your processes and the risks if the wrong decision is made?

PING MOMENTS

Time to reflect on this chapter and capture
any ideas that it has given you.

_____

_____

_____

_____

_____

_____

_____

_____

_____

_____

_____

_____

_____

_____

CHAPTER 14:

TEAM MEETINGS:
ELEMENT 10 OF 16

*"**Team Meetings**, to be effective, must start and end on time,*
An agenda sent beforehand, that keeps us all in line.
Actions duly noted, with who does what by when,
Reviewed at our next meeting, before we start again."

Category: Coactive Connections

Team DyNAmics Definition: The mechanism by which
regular communication occurs between team members
at an agreed time and with an agreed format.

Etymology: Meeting, from Old English, meaning encounter.

Newbie: What would happen if we didn't have regular team meetings?
Jules: More importantly, think about what wouldn't happen.

WHAT ARE TEAM MEETINGS?

*"You know when your team meetings are working
well, when everyone looks forward to going to them,
as opposed to trying to get out of them."*

Have you ever come away from a meeting thinking or saying to a colleague, "What a waste of time that was." I'm sure that, like me, you have. Love them or hate them, meetings are a fact of business life.

Whether you chair your team meeting or are a participant, you want to make sure that your meetings work for you and your colleagues.

Get it right and you will communicate effectively, discuss issues, share ideas, and agree actions to move things forward positively. Team meetings are an opportunity to ensure everyone hears the same message, can make decisions as a team and also hear questions or concerns that other team members may have.

Get it wrong and everyone leaves frustrated.

An article in Management Today states that, based on 500 office workers surveyed in the UK, on average workers spend 16 hours a week in meetings, with almost 25% of this time wasted. Unproductive meetings have been estimated to cost the UK economy £26 billion a year.[3]

However, meetings, especially team meetings, are an essential part of our business lives and are not going to go away, so we have to therefore ensure that they are as effective as possible and meet the needs of ALL those who attend. I've deliberately capitalised the word "all" because that is where the root of ineffective meetings occurs: people, and importantly our differing needs.

WHAT HAPPENS IN MEETINGS?

If you recall, in Chapter 2, I shared the behavioural preferences that we all have, however to varying degrees: Introversion, Extraversion, Thinking, Feeling, Sensing and Intuition. In your team meetings, you are invariably going to have a mixture of individuals with different preferences, and if these are not understood by other team members, that is when frustration occurs.

As an example, those with a preference for Extraversion like to share their ideas and views openly and therefore on occasion will tend to speak a lot. Those with a preference for Introversion, on the other hand, are comfortable to just sit and listen and absorb the communication going on around them.

Those with an Extraverted preference may therefore be thinking about those more Introverted colleagues, "Why aren't they speaking up and contributing?"

Whereas those with an Introverted preference may be thinking about their Extraverted preference colleagues, "Why don't they just shut up so someone else can add something to the conversation?"

You'll probably associate with one or the other of the above and have no doubt experienced this in meetings you've been to.

The above tends to be the biggest cause of frustrations in team meetings, however the way in which we make decisions, with either a Thinking or Feeling preference, and how we take in information, either via Sensing or Intuition, will also have an impact.

So I cannot stress enough the importance of understanding these preferences in relation to your team colleagues.

BENEFITS

1. Team **Purpose** can be reinforced to ensure the team stays focussed.
2. Enables ideas to be shared, discussed and agreed upon, to support **Decision-Making**.
3. Supports the valuing and appreciation of **Diversity**.
4. Enhances **Collaboration** due to sharing of knowledge, experience and ideas.

RED FLAGS

1. Team meetings start late or overrun on a regular basis.
2. Not everyone has the opportunity to speak up.
3. Individuals are reticent to confront and discuss issues in performance.
4. Actions from previous meetings are not reviewed at the start.

THE STORY
Meeting madness

In my early years of being in a team, the leader would call a team meeting at short notice rather than having a regular, agreed time to hold one. They did not call the team meeting due to an issue or a risk, or as part of a regular update, but purely when it suited them and when they wanted to share something with the rest of the team.

Team members would begrudgingly head along to the meeting and because it was at short notice and no agenda was shared, invariably we would not know what was to be discussed and therefore could not prepare for it. Some team members could not even attend, due to other commitments.

On the first couple of occasions that this occurred, when the topic of the team meeting was revealed by the leader some individuals would share their thoughts and ideas. However, it became quite apparent that the leader was not that interested in what others had to say, as all they wanted was to share what they wanted and expected to happen.

Whilst nothing was discussed by team members about the leader's behaviour, instinctively we all were thinking the same thing, that these meetings were simply for the benefit of the leader.

Unfortunately, due to the reputation of the leader nobody felt comfortable enough to speak up about how they were feeling about the meetings.

Quite quickly, when these meetings were called, those who were able to turn up just sat, listened and nodded their heads, knowing that anything else but compliance would result in the leader "going off on one".

The negative impact of this behaviour by the leader in relation to these impromptu team meetings had a greater impact than they no doubt could have imagined.

Due to their actions, they had lost the team and within less than three months, 75% of the team had left.

It was a lesson that I would never forget in terms of the importance of ensuring team meetings were scheduled and delivered in a way that worked for ALL the team.

THE SUGGESTION

Below are some tips that are tried and tested in making team meetings more effective for everyone.

1. Get the agenda out early. Some prefer time to gather their thoughts and prepare whereas others can often speak "off the cuff".

2. Go through the actions from the prior team meeting, so progress can be shared and actions not completed can be understood and rescheduled.

3. Go around the table to give everyone the opportunity to express their views.

4. If your team is large in terms of numbers, consider breaking out into smaller groups to discuss an idea, as some find it easier to open up in a smaller group.

5. Consider writing questions down on a piece of paper and handing them around the group for people to add their individual comments, so that nobody is put on the spot.

6. Make a note of Any Other Business, however don't go into the detail of this at the meeting; add it onto the agenda for the next meeting so people can prepare to discuss it in more depth.

7. Keep two-way communication channels open for a while after the meeting, in case someone has a great thought or idea after the meeting has finished.

FOOD FOR THOUGHT

Q1. What changes to your team meeting do you think would be beneficial?

Q2. Does everyone contribute at team meetings?

Q3. Are there actions that come out of your meetings?

Q4. Is there a positive energy to your team meetings, or is it flat?

PING MOMENTS

Time to reflect on this chapter and capture
any ideas that it has given you.

_____

_____

_____

_____

_____

_____

_____

_____

_____

_____

_____

_____

_____

_____

_____

CHAPTER 15:

PROCESSES:
ELEMENT 11 OF 16

*"**Processes** are important, to maintain consistency,*
Recorded somewhere accessible, so everyone can see.
Then if a process needs to be done by someone totally new,
They have clear instructions of what they need to do."

Category: Framework Mapping

Team DyNAmics Definition: The rules, regulations
and guidelines by which tasks are achieved.

Etymology: From the Latin, meaning a going forward.

Newbie: Why do we need to document the steps we take?
Jules: Because as well as knowing why we do things,
we also need to know how to do them.

WHAT ARE PROCESSES?

"By ensuring that each part of a process is effective,
a strong chain of excellence can be achieved."

Your Processes are the bricks and mortar of your teamwork. There will be a start point and an end point in what your team does, to achieve your Team Purpose and the goals that your team has been set.

I have worked with teams that have mapped out their processes and assigned accountability for each part to one of their team.

Equally, I have worked with teams where processes have not been mapped out and work has been undertaken in a haphazard way by different people.

I am sure that you will know which of the above is the most effective and results in the least mistakes!

In high-performing teams, invariably team members are responsible and indeed accountable for their part of each process that the team undertakes, which they then hand over to another team member and so on and so forth, until all the processes are complete.

If you can imagine you are building a tower, you start off with the first brick and then ensure that the next brick is fixed correctly next to it. Eventually, you will have built the foundation of your tower and then continue with the second row, until you have built it to the required dimensions.

The key to success is ensuring, when the next person starts to build their part of the tower, that the handover between you is effective, so that they can continue to complete their part of the job as effectively as possible.

Mapping out each of the steps in all of your processes is important, because not only will it provide you with a complete picture of what you and your team do, it will additionally have a positive impact on Accountability, because, as part of the mapping process, each step of each process should be assigned to a specific individual or individuals in your team. Therefore, if a particular part of the process fails, the team can easily identify who is accountable for that part of the process and help it to be fixed.

Risks can also be reduced when processes are mapped out. If, for some reason, a member of your team is off work, either due to illness or maybe on vacation, it means that another member of the team can undertake their part of the process, following the instructions documented.

Equally, if you have a new team member, it is much easier, when processes are mapped out, to teach them how to do them.

Another benefit is that if you have processes that are mapped out and are repeated on a regular basis, you should be able to measure how long each end-to-end process takes, because each process has stability, with each step in the process being rigorously followed and not deviated from.

When I worked for Barclays, there was a team that was dedicated to mapping out and understanding the productivity of processes, based on the efficiency and effectiveness of them. They were known by the mnemonic CWIP, standing for Clerical Work in Progress.

I remember asking one of the CWIP team, who used to go from branch to branch undertaking these studies, the benefits of their job. They used the analogy of driving your car to work. If you took the same route to work in your car each day, you could time how long each journey took and then doing the same route, at the same time each day, could work out an average, say over a fortnight, of measurements.

This would enable you to work out a start time for leaving home, to ensure that you got to work on time, as you would be able to build in some contingency to allow for hold-ups along the way.

Doing so with processes and allowing some contingency time enabled a measurement of how long different processes took, of vital importance, especially when regulatory or customer deadlines had to be hit.

In addition, if you decided to change your route to work because you thought it might be more efficient, then you would also have a benchmark time to see whether in fact it was quicker or not.

Similarly, if a part of a process is changed, either to try to make it more efficient, linked maybe to some work that you and your team have been doing on Transformation or to comply with new rules or regulations, you will then be able to understand whether that change has a positive or negative impact, in how long it takes.

Ultimately, if the change is because of new rules or regulations that need to be complied with to remain within the law, then there is nothing you can do about it. If these changes increase the length of a process, however, at least you know that they do and therefore what, if any, knock-on effects on other processes this may have.

So hopefully, you will be able to recognise and appreciate the value of mapping your processes. The other key considerations when doing so are how to do this, who will be involved and how will you document each process. This is obviously something for you and your team to agree on.

Ultimately, in mapping out your processes, you are trying to create what I like to call a Chain of Excellence, ensuring that each end-to-end process is completed effectively and efficiently.

BENEFITS

1. Increases effectiveness and efficiency, whilst supporting **Accountability**.
2. Helps **Transformation**, by enabling the team to test whether solutions reduce the time taken to undertake something.

3. Enhances the **Decision-Making** process, due to knowing who is responsible for certain processes.
4. Supports **Commitment** in individuals and pride in the part they play and in what they deliver.

RED FLAGS

1. The same process or processes go wrong on a regular basis.
2. Individuals blame each other when something goes wrong.
3. Customer complaints are frequent or stay at a high number.
4. Critical deadlines are missed on a recurring basis.

THE STORY
The Chain of Excellence

My wife and I have always had a love for food and whenever we have been able, we have booked meals at restaurants with a good reputation. The majority of these have been in the UK, however we have also sought out restaurants with a good reputation when we have been on our travels.

In addition to the excellent food, they have all had one thing in common: an excellence in their processes to ensure that, as customers, we have had the best experience possible.

When I have worked with teams, when they have had issues with their processes, I always introduce the concept of creating a "Chain of Excellence". Let me explain using a visit to one of our favourite restaurants, The Kings Arms in Christchurch, Dorset, where the restaurant service is overseen by Michelin-starred Chef Patron Alex Aitken and his amazing team.

Just prior to Christmas 2020, my wife and I had booked a five-course festive menu with wine pairing with each course. We had booked the event online, leaving our details, and a couple of days later, I received a call to confirm my booking, the time and to take a deposit to secure the booking. I was also asked whether either my wife or I had any allergies. The woman on the call was both informative about the event and extremely pleasant, finishing off with, "We look forward to seeing you and your wife next week."

On the evening of the event, we arrived at the restaurant about 15 minutes before our allocated time. We were greeted warmly at the door and asked to scan the NHS Track and Trace QR code and then to have our temperature taken, using an electronic temperature screen that they had installed.

With the safety measures completed, we were then ushered to the check-in area, where our greeter handed us over to another member of the team, after wishing us both an enjoyable evening.

Once we had been checked in, we were asked whether we wished to have our coats taken, prior to being seated. My wife and I were then introduced to our waitress for the evening. She greeted us using our names, which she had heard the check-in staff using.

She led us through the restaurant to the seat that they had allocated us. Our waitress then asked us whether we were happy with our table, or whether we preferred to sit at another table. The table we had been allocated, however, was perfect.

She then asked us whether we wanted some water for the table, giving us a choice of bottled still or sparkling, or tap water. Once we had let her know, she said she would come back with it and the menu.

The festive menu was five courses, which had already been set, however our waitress took us through each course and then said that although it had been noted at the time of the original booking that we did not have any allergies, she just wanted to check whether anything had changed or indeed, if there was something on the menu that we did not like.

After confirming that the menu was great and that nothing had changed regarding allergies, our waitress introduced us to the sommelier. He let us know that he would give us some history about each of the wines that were paired with each course and why they had been chosen.

After a reasonable amount of time, which allowed my wife and I to have a chat, our sommelier returned and poured the first of the wines, to go with our starter. He shared his knowledge of the wine in an engaging way and also why he had chosen it. Just as he finished, our waitress appeared with our starter.

The food was excellent, and each course was presented beautifully. Artichoke, Truffle and Chestnut Soup, Smoked Salmon Canneloni, Hake Fillet, Stuffed Breast of Turkey, Brandy Soaked Christmas Pudding. The chefs had done an incredible job.

Wines from France, New Zealand and Spain complemented each of the courses.

After our third course, our waitress enquired whether we wanted a break and if so, for how long. My wife and I agreed that a ten-minute respite from the culinary delights would be appreciated. Almost to the second, our fourth course appeared.

We finished off our meal with a cup of coffee, a cappuccino for my wife and double espresso for myself and complimentary after-meal mints. Perfect.

Our waitress and sommelier both asked whether we had enjoyed ourselves, which we wholeheartedly had, at which point I asked for our bill.

I had noticed that at the bottom of the menu there was a lovely touch. It said, "If you have enjoyed the service this evening, a 10% service charge is payable at your discretion." A wonderful touch, rather than having it automatically added to your bill. Everything had been superb and my wife and I gladly paid 20% for the service.

We were escorted to the check-in desk by our waitress and before we left, the person at check-in asked us whether we had had an enjoyable evening and whether there was anything that we would have changed or that could have been better. Absolutely nothing, it was perfect, we replied.

The above is a brilliant example of a Chain of Excellence in processes. It involved five different people, four of whom had face-to-face contact with my wife and I, and additionally the chefs and their teams who prepared, cooked and plated our food.

This not only takes an enormous amount of teamwork but also a detailed understanding of each element of the process, from start to finish, and is something that needs to be reviewed and refined on a regular basis, to ensure that the Chain of Excellence remains strong.

Now, the main issue with processes, more often than not, occurs during the handover to another person. If a process is going to fail, this is when it will occur. The restaurant team, as you will have read, had this completely nailed.

My wife and I have experienced the same high level of service, food and "Chain of Excellence" at Alex's other chain of restaurants, The Jetty, and if you are ever in the Hampshire/Dorset area, I would thoroughly recommend checking these out or The Kings Arms that I have mentioned.

THE SUGGESTION

My suggestion is that, if you have not already done so, you start out by mapping your critical processes. Those processes that, if not completed effectively, correctly or on time, will have a major impact on the products or services that you and your company deliver or put you at breach of legal requirements.

When I have worked with teams on this, I have often use flipcharts or Post-it notes as a starting point. At a high level, capture a top-level description and brief information about each step of the process and also capture the name of the person who is accountable for that part of it.

You have then got something visual to work through. For each step, you should be asking the question, "Is this step necessary?" If the answer is yes, the second question should be, "Is it being completed in the most efficient way possible?" If the answer to this is also yes, then you can move on to the next step of the process. I can almost guarantee that you will find redundant parts of a process or ineffective steps that have been added over the years.

With one team I was supporting, I challenged them on why they were completing certain steps in a process which resulted in a report being generated for another department.

When they asked the other department if they needed the report, they advised them that they did not and that it had not been needed for several years. When it turned up in their inbox, they just deleted it but had never thought to mention that it was not required!

Over time, as people move in and out of teams, if we are not careful, processes can be added to or indeed undertaken for no current reason and before you know it, you and your team are undertaking tasks that are either extremely ineffective, or indeed no longer need to be completed anymore, so reviewing your processes on a regular basis can have huge benefits.

Finally, remember that whilst some people have a learning style that means they are quite happy to read a document or manual to learn a process, others have a learning style which is hands on, learning by doing, so it is important to remember this when new members of the team are asked to learn a different process.

When I used to train facilitators, I would explain to them the process they were about to learn, supplemented by a document that detailed the process, and then I would demonstrate that process to them and when they felt comfortable, shadow them as they undertook it. When, and only when, they felt comfortable and I also felt comfortable, would I be happy with them undertaking it themselves and being accountable for it.

FOOD FOR THOUGHT

Q1. When was the last time that you and your team reviewed your end-to-end processes, mapping them out?

Q2. Where are your critical processes documented, so if you were unavailable someone else in your team could complete them?

Q3. In an emergency, would you know where to look to find out how to undertake a particular process?

Q4. When someone suggests doing something in a different way, how do you know it is more effective and efficient than the way in which you do it already?

PING MOMENTS

Time to reflect on this chapter and capture
any ideas that it has given you.

_____

_____

_____

_____

_____

_____

_____

_____

_____

_____

_____

_____

_____

_____

_____

_____

CHAPTER 16

ENVIRONMENT:
ELEMENT 12 OF 16

"Everybody feels much better, working in a vibrant place,
*As a positive **Environment** will put a smile upon your face,*
So whether working remotely, or when we're all together,
Our team should be a great place to
work, for all and for forever."

Category: Creative Interactions

Team DyNAmics Definition: The atmosphere and
culture that exists in the working environment.

Etymology: From Old French, meaning surrounding.

Newbie: What is the best working environment?
Jules: One where we all feel valued, and our needs are met.

WHAT IS ENVIRONMENT?

"When the working environment and culture are positive,
you can see and feel it, without anything being said."

Environment is the working culture that exists in your team. It is what creates the atmosphere that you work in on a daily basis. It is what leads to individuals and your team overall enjoying what you do and delivering your goals.

I remember being on vacation in Saint Lucia, with my wife, when we came across an elderly Saint Lucian man at a market. We got chatting about where we were from, which in turn got us chatting about him and his life. He talked about his family, including his wife and children, and his job. He then came out with a wonderful quotation about him being content and enjoying life. He simply smiled and said, "Happy wife, happy life."

This resonated with me and got me thinking about team members being content and enjoying working in the team and the quotation "A happy team delivers the dream" popped into my head.

What I mean by this is that in those teams where a positive working environment has been created, the chances of delivering against your **Team Purpose**, and indeed your **Vision**, are greatly enhanced.

Even in teams that have goals that are a matter of life and death, such as the blue light services or armed forces, they invariably create a positive working environment, recognising how critical this is to their success. They have a camaraderie, a mutual trust and friendship, that goes above and beyond just working with a colleague.

As a facilitator, regularly, when I have worked with teams, within as little as 15 minutes of starting to work with them I can pick up whether they have a positive working environment, based on how they interact with me and their colleagues, the stories that they tell about their teamwork and quite frequently, the affectionate nicknames that they have for each other.

Now, I mention nicknames, however you will see I have prefixed it with the word "affectionate". Nicknames in teams work, provided the person who the nickname relates to recognises it and appreciates it for what it is: a sign of affection.

I have worked with and in teams where there has been someone nicknamed Lightbulb, because they always came up with lots of ideas. Gluey, as they always stuck to the rules and procedures. Marathon, because they would always go the extra mile to help colleagues and the team. The key was that they all loved their nicknames as they reflected a positive characteristic trait that they demonstrated.

BENEFITS

1. Increases **Trust** between individuals, as team members get to know each other much better.
2. Enhances the **Commitment** to the team by individuals, by increasing pride in the team.
3. Boosts the desire and will to **Collaborate**, as it is about team success.
4. Promotes a positive can-do attitude, when trying to achieve the goals and **Purpose** of the team.

RED FLAGS

1. A flat atmosphere exists. Not many smiles or laughter. Heads down, getting on with the job.
2. Individuals are not prepared to go the extra mile to help colleagues or step in when an emergency occurs.
3. Very little or no social interaction outside of work.
4. Individuals very much keep themselves to themselves.

THE STORY
The elephant in the room

On a number of occasions, I have been called in to work with teams to "firefight or help fix things" and this was a case in point. A newly incumbent leader of a leadership team asked me to work with them and their team to try to overcome the "legacy culture" that they had inherited.

They informed me that the team, which totalled 15, had been formed 6 months previously, from 4 separate leadership teams that worked quite independently of each other.

On the first day of the programme, as soon as I walked into the room I noticed that there was almost a hush in the room, no vibrancy or buzz of conversation that is often the case with many teams that I work with.

I also noticed that the leaders had split themselves into four groups, each standing in each of the four corners of the room. In each of the groups, there were hushed conversations going on.

I introduced myself and grabbed a coffee and made my way to each of the groups to introduce myself. As I came up to each group in turn, so the conversation stopped. It became quite apparent that each group was talking about one or all of the other groups.

When I got the team to sit down at the cabaret-style tables, I noticed that they all sat in the same groups.

The elephant in the room needed to be addressed. I first asked them whether they were a team. There was some hesitancy before confirmation was forthcoming.

So, to test this out, I asked each of them to write down the Purpose of their team and was not surprised to get many different answers. So my first task was to help them to create their own Team Purpose. If you wish to read more about Team Purpose and how to create yours, if you do not have one, please refer to Chapter 5 in this book that explains how to do it.

I then set about exploring their team culture. Now quite often, when teams are formed from other teams, unless a concerted effort is put into creating a new culture, legacy cultures will be referred to and you will hear stories shared about "what we used to do in our team". It is as though team members get stuck in the past.

Now, based on my experience, to create a new culture you need to resolve, involve and evolve.

You firstly need to resolve any issues that currently exist and find ways to overcome them.

Then involve everyone in creating a framework for the new culture and ways of working. In doing so you will get buy-in and commitment to it.

Finally, creating a new culture will not happen overnight and you need to adopt new ways of working, incorporating new ideas and practical solutions, so that the new culture evolves over time.

Below is a suggestion based on the work that I completed with the team to help them to create the positive working environment.

THE SUGGESTION

One of the activities that I undertake with teams to ensure that there is a positive working environment is called "Keep, Ditch, Use, Create".

As you can no doubt imagine, it is all about making sure you keep what is working well, ditch or stop what is not working well, use things that have worked well in previous teams that you have worked in and create new ways of working that you and your team agree are of value.

I use the above as a framework to get the team to discuss the following areas that help to create and agree a positive working environment that works for them.

- What values do we want to uphold in our team?
- How do we want to behave towards each other?
- What rules do we want to have in how we work?
- How do we want to celebrate success?
- How do we want to interact with each other socially?
- How do we want to get to know each other personally?

Whilst the above list is not exhaustive, invariably it will generate discussions about other aspects of your working environment that you can also incorporate.

Whatever you come up with, the key to success and making it happen is that the majority, if not all of your team, buy into and commit to what has been agreed.

FOOD FOR THOUGHT

Q1. What would you say are the positive attributes of your team culture?

Q2. What are the negative aspects of the working environment in your team?

Q3. What do you do when your team achieve a milestone or have success?

Q4. What things do you do socially as a team, outside of office hours?

PING MOMENTS

Time to reflect on this chapter and capture
any ideas that it has given you.

_____

_____

_____

_____

_____

_____

_____

_____

_____

_____

_____

_____

_____

CHAPTER 17:

VISION:
ELEMENT 13 OF 16

*"Our **Vision** is the future, what we want to see,*
Going from where we are today, to where we want to be.
Stretching yet achievable, so it will inspire,
Individuals and our team, to raise performance higher."

Category: Strategic Action

Team DyNAmics Definition: The longer term, aspirational
view of what the team would like to achieve.

Etymology: From the Latin, the act of seeing.

Newbie: Why do we need a Vision?
Jules: Without one we may be good, however
may not strive to be even better.

WHAT IS VISION?

*"The greatest accomplishments come from those
who turn a dream of the future into reality."*

A Team Vision should be aspirational, future orientated and a statement of intent. It is a longer term view of what you want to do, or be recognised for as a team.

A Team Vision statement should inspire and motivate your team to achieve something above and beyond what you currently do at this moment in time. It should also be clear and easy to remember.

Quite often a Team Vision statement will be a short sentence, also known as a tagline or strapline.

It is worthwhile pointing out that it should not be confused with your Team Purpose Statement, which is operational and short term, and sometimes referred to as a Mission Statement.

A good example of something that combines both Purpose and Vision, that a lot of people will be able to relate to, comes from the hit TV and film series, *Star Trek*.

This statement was narrated by James T. Kirk, captain of the *Starship Enterprise*, at the start of each episode of the original TV series. The purpose element was about exploring strange new worlds, new life and new civilisations and the vision element was about boldly going where no man had gone before. The purpose was operational and short term, whilst the vision was aspirational and future orientated.

Below are a few more examples of vision statements from well-known companies and brands:

Zoom: Video communications empowering people to accomplish more.

LinkedIn: Creating economic opportunity for every member of the global workforce.

Google: To provide access to the world's information in one click.

Amazon: To be Earth's most customer-centric company, where customers can find and discover anything they might want to buy online.

PayPal: To build the Web's most convenient, secure, cost-effective payment solution.

BBC: To enrich people's lives with programmes and services that inform, educate and entertain.

Marks and Spencer: To be the standard against which others are measured.

My suggestion would be to seek out the vision statements of well-known companies or brands that you know and share them with your team as examples, so that clarity of understanding of what a vision statement is can be achieved before you and your team create yours.

And remember, a vision statement should be aspirational and future orientated, whereas a purpose statement is short term and operational.

BENEFITS

1. Gets the team to **Reflect** on where they are now and where they want to get to.
2. Provides team members with an understanding of how their **Roles & Skills** will help to achieve the team's Vision.
3. Helps with longer term **Planning**, that goes beyond achieving short-term operational goals.
4. Enhances individual **Commitment** to what the team is aspiring to become.

RED FLAGS

1. Little or no sense of pride in what the team does or wants to be recognised for.
2. The team merely focuses on short-term goals and "doing their job", without stretching themselves.
3. Innovation and new ways of working are not explored.
4. The longer term is rarely discussed at team meetings, the focus being on current day-to-day activities.

THE STORY
A vision for finance

If you recall, in the earlier chapter about Purpose (Chapter 5), I shared the story of how I had helped a finance team to create a Team Purpose Statement, as the one that they had was bland, uninspiring and did nothing for their credibility with other departments. Here is what they created.

The Finance Team exists to ensure the timely delivery of value-adding financial and accounting data and key performance indicators to our global business units, which enables them to make informed future investment decisions that deliver tangible benefits to our customers, staff and company.

I continued to work with the team, over a period of time, on various elements of their teamwork, one of which was to create a Vision Statement.

What they eventually agreed upon was the following:

To be recognised as the experts in all things financial.

The key for them was being recognised by other departments for their expertise.

If you read "The Suggestion" below, you will understand how they created it.

Finally, as another example that I practise what I preach, my Business Purpose Statement is as follows:

Ngagementworks exists to engage individuals and motivate teams, helping them transform and achieve even greater success, through more effective teamwork.

My Business Vision Statement is:

To be the "go-to" business for teams wishing to enhance their teamwork and effectiveness.

So, it is important to have a Purpose Statement that is short term and operational, and a Vision that is longer term and aspirational.

THE SUGGESTION

Creating a Vision for your team can be a fascinating activity to undertake, as it taps into our creativity.

Firstly, I would suggest that you get clarity in terms of what a Team Vision is by sharing some of the information that I have shared above.

It is a good idea to provide examples, so do use the ones that I have mentioned, or indeed seek out some of your own that I am sure you will easily find using the internet.

Once you have done the above, get individuals to either work individually or in groups and come up with as many Vision statements as they can. I often get them to write them on a Post-it note and then put them all on a flipchart.

Let everyone have a good look at what has been written and give each team member three votes for their favourites. Get them to put their mark beside the three that they have chosen.

In doing so, you should end up with possibly a shortlist of two or maybe three that the majority of the team like.

Have another round of voting, with each team member being allowed to only vote for one, which should hopefully get you to be able to choose a final one.

A good sense check here is whether it is congruent with your Team Purpose. Hopefully it will be.

Once the above is achieved, it is time to bring it to life.

Get your team to imagine that they are in the future and they are succeeding in delivering against your Vision.

Divide a flipchart into four quadrants and head up each one Doing, Saying, Feeling and Thinking.

Get each person to write down individually, on a Post-it note, what people will be Doing, Saying, Feeling and Thinking about the team because you are delivering against your Vision (some of you will remember that I use the same technique as part of the BEPART model, which I have already shared earlier in the book). There should be one comment for each quadrant per person. Then get them to stick their comments in the appropriate quadrant.

Once everyone has done this, it is useful to go through them all with your team, to see whether there are similarities or differences in team members' comments.

Finally, have a discussion about how you will ensure that your Vision stays in people's minds.

- Who will you share it with outside of your team?
- How will you bring your Vision to life?
- Is there an image that would bring your Vision to life?
- Will you use it in communication both internal and external to your team?

FOOD FOR THOUGHT

Q1. Does your team have a Vision statement and if so does everyone know what it is?

Q2. If you have a Vision statement, does it align with your Team Purpose?

Q3. When was the last time your Vision was reviewed to ensure it is still relevant?

Q4. Is your Vision shared with new team members, as part of their induction?

PING MOMENTS

Time to reflect on this chapter and capture
any ideas that it has given you.

_____

_____

_____

_____

_____

_____

_____

_____

_____

_____

_____

_____

_____

_____

CHAPTER 18

DIVERSITY:
ELEMENT 14 OF 16

*"**Diversity** and respect, so we can celebrate,*
Our individuality, and how we operate,
It's just the way we are; there's no right or wrong,
So let's appreciate our differences, so we can get along."

Category: Coactive Connections

Team DyNAmics Definition: The recognition and appreciation of differences between individual team members in their behaviours, styles and skills.

Etymology: From the Latin, meaning turned different ways.

Newbie: Is it good enough just to recognise we are all different?
Jules: Recognition is just the start. Appreciation is when the team can use these differences positively.

WHAT IS DIVERSITY?

*"By embracing every aspect of each person in
the team, we can feel truly appreciated for who
we are and what we bring to the team."*

Below is a definition of diversity which I believe is a good example of what diversity is generally recognised as being.

Diversity is the range of human differences, including but not limited to race, ethnicity, gender, gender identity, sexual orientation, age, social class, physical ability or attributes, religious or ethical values system, national origin, and political beliefs.[4]

The majority of organisations focus their efforts on education and policies that are non-discriminatory based on the above. This is highly commendable and needed, yet I believe that they overlook a form of discrimination that causes just as much, if not more damage than the others mentioned.

What I believe is overlooked or, indeed, not given the attention that it deserves is something that causes people more heartache, stress and time off, and that is a lack of understanding and appreciation of behavioural diversity. This is the recognition that we are all different in how we behave, make decisions and communicate, due to our personality or behavioural traits.

Hopefully, having read Chapter 2 about the importance of knowing **WHO** is in your team, you will have a better understanding of behavioural diversity and how to use this positively.

Now, turning to the other types of diversity mentioned above, they also need to be discussed openly within your team because, if there is an issue, this can rapidly escalate and turn into something more sinister, namely bullying.

This sort of behaviour is simply **NOT ACCEPTABLE**, however it still goes on and, in some businesses, is still commonplace. So, why don't people speak up?

Here are some of the reasons I've heard.

"I did it once, never again."

"There's no support or person to turn to for help."

"They're more senior than me."

"I'm fearful of what impact it'll have on my career."

"Nothing gets done about it."

"Nobody else speaks up."

"I'm scared of the consequences."

"I've seen what has happened to others."

I'm sure there are many other reasons as well, however more often than not people don't speak up because of **FEAR**. Fear of what may, or indeed, may not happen to change the situation. However, if we do not speak up, nothing will change.

Now, based on who is in your team, some or all of the areas of diversity may need to be discussed and I will share this in my suggestion below.

BENEFITS

1. A greater range of views and perspectives, leading to better ideas and practical solutions, aiding **Transformation**.
2. Discussions in **Team Meetings** are more productive and wide-ranging.

3. Boosts **Commitment** to the team and what it needs to achieve.
4. Enhances **Communication** by recognising and appreciating different communication needs.

RED FLAGS

1. Lack of engagement from team members and low morale.
2. Individuals are attacked personally, based on who they are.
3. Team members do not praise others in the team.
4. Individuals will not collaborate with certain team members.

THE STORY
The Bedouin tent

I had been working with a company in the UK for a few years, after one of the directors had seen me speak at a conference. I had worked with many teams in the company, including leadership, operational and project teams. The teamwork sessions I had facilitated, combined with the behavioural profiling, had delivered many positive benefits, including better communication, increased effectiveness in teamwork and leadership of teams, to name a few.

Then I received a call from the director, who told me that he had a mission for me. It sounded ominous, however I listened to what he told me.

The company, in partnership with two others, was undertaking a large project, planned to take approximately two years to deliver. The project team consisted of almost equal numbers of British, French and German project managers, 30 in total.

The project was two months in and not going well, with a lot of friction between the three nationality groups, which was having a negative impact on decision-making, communication, team meetings, roles and skills, accountability and trust.

The director asked me to check my calendar for specific dates at the end of May, which I confirmed were free.

He then asked me to book out those dates in my diary. It was at this point that he told me that the team were based in Saudi Arabia and that he would send me details of where to send my passport to get a fast-track visa.

The final thing the director revealed in that initial conversation was the fact that he did not want the training to take place in a hotel, with air conditioning, as they were used to this.

He reminded me that, during one of the sessions I had previously facilitated, I had mentioned that undertaking training outside of the office, or in an unusual setting, had benefits, in terms of engagement and retention of the learning, due to the experience.

As such, he had arranged that the two-day training session he wanted me to facilitate would take place in a Bedouin tent, about one hour from the capital, Riyadh, in the middle of the Saudi Arabian desert. Due to the lack of electricity, this would require me to create the presentation materials using flipcharts!

With my passport duly stamped with my work visa, I headed to Heathrow for the flight to Riyadh and my first ever visit to Saudi Arabia.

On arrival, my first night was spent in the hotel being used by the project team. It gave me an opportunity to have a chat with them. Interestingly, the team members were sitting in their respective nationality groups.

This enabled me to have a chat with each group, to potentially unearth some of the things that were causing the friction.

At the end of my chat with the three groups, it became clear that the biggest barrier was caused by national stereotyping.

The Germans and French did not want the Brits in charge because they felt that this would mean endless meetings and discussions.

The French and Brits did not want the Germans in charge as they felt that they would make decisions without consultation with others.

The Germans and Brits did not want the French to be in charge, as they thought that things would move forward too slowly, as they tried to get the agreement of everyone to take action.

I had experienced stereotyping before, based on regional accents in the UK, however I found the national stereotyping fascinating.

Having this additional information direct from the project team members enabled me to think on my feet as to how to break down this stereotyping and, instead, get them to value and appreciate the diversity of individuals.

The following morning, after a hearty breakfast, we gathered outside the hotel and were soon greeted by eight people carriers. It was not long before we were heading out towards the Saudi Arabian desert. Soon the modern buildings of Riyadh had disappeared, and the straight road was flanked on either side by desert.

After about an hour, a black dot appeared on the horizon, surrounded by the desert sand. As our convoy sped on, the black dot became bigger and bigger. When we were about a mile away, it became apparent that this was our home for the next couple of days.

The people carriers went off road and as we got closer, we saw that there was one black Bedouin tent, open down the whole of one side, with a smaller white tent beside it and a couple of white plastic telephone-box-like structures raised up on concrete blocks.

We were later to find out that the white tent was a cookhouse, from which our food for the next couple of days would be prepared by a Saudi father and his two sons. The two white telephone-box-like structures were in fact dual purpose. They were both a toilet, which also included a shower.

The reason that they were raised up from the sand on concrete blocks was, we were advised, to stop vipers and scorpions from crawling into them!

The Bedouin tent was to be our training room, dining room, living room and bedroom for the next two days. We were each given a sleeping bag and told that as we were sleeping on the carpeted floor of the tent, we should pull the drawstrings tight before going to sleep to stop any local wildlife from crawling into our sleeping bags to join us!

After a traditional Saudi breakfast of strong coffee, honey and sesame coated dates, I set about breaking down the barriers that had been created by the national stereotyping.

As you will have picked up, whenever I am able to I use four or a multiple of four in whatever I do, because it is a number that our brains can easily remember and store.

So I started off by facilitating a session called "Find Four". I briefed everyone that they had to find four people who had a connection with them, but not from their nationality group. It also had to be four different people and four different connections. When they found a person, they had to write down their name and also the connection.

The connection could be anything they liked, a favourite film or pop group, whether they were left or right-handed, the number of siblings they had, what sign of the zodiac they were born under. Favourite food, favourite holiday destinations, biggest fear, absolutely anything.

Quite often, I challenge groups to find four people as quickly as possible and for the person who does it first to let me know, however this time I felt it appropriate to let things play out.

It was great to observe the conversations that were going on, watching people writing down names, the connections being made and importantly, the laughter coming from all corners of the Bedouin tent.

Once everyone had found four connections, I undertook a short debrief, exploring such things as the most unusual connections.

I did not want to go much further at this stage, for a particular reason. That afternoon, we explored behavioural differences, with each person receiving their own unique profile. I then arranged the groups into their dominant colour behavioural preferences and got them to discuss and then share the strengths and value to the team that their lead colour energy brought to the team.

Those who led with Red said things like getting things done at pace, making decisions quickly when needed, keeping the end goal in mind.

Those who led with Yellow mentioned their ability to think creatively and come up with ideas, verbal communication and ease in building relationships with others.

Those who led with Green mentioned their ability to create harmony, their listening skills, and empathy with others, by considering possible decisions and how these decisions might make others feel.

Those who led with Blue energy took pride in their planning capabilities, ability to spot risks and need to gather information, so that the right decision was made.

It was at this point that I took the opportunity to explore these connections, based on different behavioural preferences.

That evening, the mood in the Bedouin tent, as we ate the goat and spiced rice that had been served up, was one of positivity and laughter. I noticed that the groups based on nationality were no more, with individuals mixing with many people in the team. It was a joy to behold.

That night, most people slept fitfully for two reasons. Firstly due to the temperature which, since we were in the desert, was still 40°C at 6 pm, and did not drop much more during the night and secondly, the thought of what creatures might be near us as we lay on the carpeted floor of the tent.

As the whole length of the tent was open, the only consolation was the beauty of staring at the stars and constellations displayed in the beautiful night sky without manmade light pollution, a memory that will stay with me forever.

The final activity that I undertook to further increase their appreciation of diversity through their common connections was to start by randomly choosing one member of the team, who stood in the middle of the tent. Everyone else formed a circle around them.

I then asked for another member of the team to put up their hand, if they had a connection with that person, via their conversations or their behavioural profiles. A lot of hands went up, so I chose one person and asked them to stand beside that person and share with everyone else what their connection was.

Once this had occurred, I asked the group if anyone had a connection with the second person and we repeated the process. One by one, individuals moved from the outer circle to the inner circle, until everyone was part of the inner circle.

I facilitated a final debrief based on what barriers the activities had removed, what value it had provided to the team and what they would do differently in the future, which they captured on a flipchart and owned.

This was a simple, yet effective way of breaking down stereotypes, appreciating diversity through commonalities in their lives and behaviours, and building trust between individuals.

A few weeks after I returned to the UK, the director, who had not been part of the training, had gone to Saudi to see how things were going. I received a wonderful email saying that he could not believe the positive change in the team and how things had got back on track extremely quickly thereafter.

THE SUGGESTION

By all means use the example above to explore diversity or you may want to consider this one.

I call this activity "Recognising and Appreciating Diversity".

Because each team is different, based on who is in the team first of all you need to understand which areas of diversity you need to focus on.

This can be achieved quite simply, by asking team members what type of diversity is relevant to them, based on who they are.

It could be that one of the team says that gender diversity is important to them.

At this point, get them to explain why it is important to them and what their colleagues can do to not only recognise but also, importantly, appreciate this type of diversity.

It may be that it is important to others in the team, so listen to what they have got to say.

Once a particular area of diversity has been discussed, open up conversation about other areas that may be relevant to individuals within the team and explore these, as above.

Eventually, you should have discussed all the areas of diversity that are relevant to your team.

Whatever you have discussed, make sure it is captured, shared and reviewed on a regular basis, especially as new team members join and others leave your team.

You can take it one stage further by creating a Diversity Charter. This can be anything that the team agree upon, provided that at the heart of it, it is about firstly recognising diversity within individuals and secondly, valuing and appreciating these differences to the benefit of individuals and the team overall.

FOOD FOR THOUGHT

Q1.   Have you seen or experienced discrimination in your team, based on who people are?

Q2.   Do differences of opinion cause conflict or are they appreciated as helping to find the best solution or idea?

Q3.   Do you have examples where your colleagues have appreciated you for who you are and what you bring to the team?

Q4.   When was the last time that your team dedicated some time to exploring diversity between individuals?

PING MOMENTS

Time to reflect on this chapter and capture
any ideas that it has given you.

_____

_____

_____

_____

_____

_____

_____

_____

_____

_____

_____

_____

_____

_____

_____

_____

CHAPTER 19

REFLECTION:
ELEMENT 15 OF 16

*"**Reflection** is important, a chance to stop, look back,*
What's gone well in what we've done,
and what's taken us off track.
To continue to learn and improve are the things we need,
If we are to perform at our best, and as a team succeed."

Category: Framework Mapping

Team DyNAmic Definition: Reviewing what has happened within your team, to learn from things that have gone well and not so well.

Etymology: From the Latin, meaning to bend backwards.

Newbie: What is the point of spending time
looking at what we have done?
Jules: To keep doing what works and to change what doesn't.

WHAT IS REFLECTION?

*"By shining a light on what we have done in the past,
we can illuminate a better way to go in the future."*

Sometimes, I wonder whether our brains have been wiped clean when we are in work mode as we seem to lose some of the abilities that come to us naturally outside of work.

This certainly seems to be the case when it comes to time for the team to reflect. As individuals, as part of our wellbeing, we often take time out to reflect on what we have done, which helps us to decide whether to continue to do things how we have done them in the past, or whether it is beneficial to change how we do things in the future.

Over the years, I have come across a lot of teams that literally just get their heads down when in work and do exactly that, work, work, work, without any time out to reflect on what they are doing and whether it is beneficial and working well for the team.

There may be pressure from stakeholders or customers to deliver outputs by an agreed milestone, an expectation that a certain degree of quality needs to be delivered on time, or a slippage in budgeted costs that needs to be reined back.

Whatever it is, many teams do not say **STOP** and set aside quality time to reflect on what they do. Invariably, those that do not continue to make the same mistakes that they have done in the past and do not optimise their effectiveness and efficiency.

Just as we are advised to take regular stops on a car journey, especially if it is over a number of hours, equally as a team you should be regularly stopping on your journey to achieving your goals and objectives.

Reflection enables a team to catch their breath, reflect on what they have done, to highlight what they may need to stop doing, to celebrate what is working well and they need to continue to do, and finally discuss and agree practical ideas that they need to implement and start to do, that would make things even better than they are now.

In summary, what does our team need to:

- Stop doing
- Continue doing
- Start doing?

BENEFITS

1. It ensures that **Processes** undertaken by the team are relevant.
2. Helps to keep efficiency and effectiveness at high levels and the team fit for **Purpose**.
3. Supports what the team needs to do in the future to achieve their **Vision**.
4. Reinforces interdependencies between team members and aids **Collaboration**.

RED FLAGS

1. The team focusses solely on hitting targets and deadlines.
2. There is little or no challenge on how the team undertakes tasks or processes.
3. Mistakes are not seen as an opportunity to learn, so that they do not occur in the future.
4. Ideas are infrequently shared at team meetings to enhance effectiveness.

THE STORY
Effective reflection

I was working as part of a team that had monthly, quarterly, half-yearly and yearly regulatory requirements that needed to be delivered to remain legal and continue to operate under licence.

The pressure was constant, with one month rolling into the next. Regulatory requirements needed to be delivered by the tenth working day of the following month and after this had been completed, the team was focussed on delivering the following months, which loomed large.

Throw in holiday entitlements and sickness and the team I worked in was always under constant pressure and it was no surprise that sickness levels were high, due to the amount of stress that we were under.

One day, due to the sickness of a team member, I had to undertake their duties. Due to the regulatory nature of our jobs, one of the things that we had was written processes and procedures.

I began to work my way methodically through them. Reports had to be run on various computer systems, the output had to be analysed and spreadsheets populated with key figures and data.

The outputs then had to be handed on to other members of the team, to add other data, before eventually being handed back. This took about two days before it was then handed on to another team in another department by an agreed date in the working month.

Being the inquisitive type, when I handed it to a team member in the other department I asked the question, "What is this data used for?"

The person said that they did not know, as they were quite new to the team and department, however they would make enquiries. After about a week, I chased up the other person to find out whether they had an answer for me.

They replied positively and told me that the report was no longer required. In fact the report had not been required for the last two years. Regulations had changed over this period of time, as had staff on their team and the notes in their procedures had last been updated by a team member who had long since left, saying that the report should simply be filed.

So my question had proved positive, as it meant that two days' work for our team had been recovered.

I shared what I had done at our next team meeting and the team agreed that it would be a good idea to investigate all of the processes that we undertook, to ensure that they were both needed and still fit for purpose.

Rather than undertaking this in a big bang approach, which would have required a mini project team to be created, we agreed that it should be completed as we went through our daily, weekly, monthly and quarterly procedures.

This generated some additional ideas that benefited the team.

One of the team suggested we use a whiteboard to share any successes. Each process that was no longer required would be added to the whiteboard, together with the amount of time saved.

In our written procedures, we also added some additional information including the date and by whom the process had been reviewed and depending on the importance of the process, a date when it would be reviewed in the future.

By the end of the quarter, our team had streamlined most of our processes and in doing so, saved the time equivalent to one person working full time. Quite significant when you consider that we were a team of ten.

I hope, based on the above, that you can appreciate the value of stopping what your team is doing and reflecting on what is working well and what needs to be changed.

Whilst facilitating some team development more recently, I was discussing the importance of the need to reflect with a team.

These discussions got the team to explore some of the things that were high priority for them to investigate, of which one was a process that was in place relating to a particular emergency that the team might face.

As I was facilitating the session, I suggested that we use it as a real case study. One of the team went off and brought back the manual in which the written procedures were.

In case of emergency, a solution had to be delivered within 5 minutes.

The first thing I asked was how many pages were in the procedure manual. After a quick count, it turned out there were 32 pages, 32 pages that had to be read and actioned, so a solution could be delivered in 5 minutes. I think you can understand where I am going with this!

Over the years bits and pieces had been added to the manual by various team members, both past and present, without anyone taking a detailed look at it.

A week after the session, I received an email from one of the team to let me know that the process had been reviewed and the procedure manual amended, and was now 4 pages in total, which meant that in an emergency, a solution could easily be actioned within 5 minutes.

THE SUGGESTION

Set aside some dedicated time when your team can all get together, stop doing your daily tasks and reflect upon what individuals and your team are doing.

Often I talk about "nibbling the elephant". Basically, you cannot eat a whole elephant in one sitting, so you need to take bite-size chunks, over a period of time.

It is the same when you reflect on what you do. Do not reflect on many areas of what your team do; rather focus on either the critical tasks that you do, those that are the most time consuming, or those things that keep going wrong.

Map them out, which should be relatively easy if you have undertaken the suggestion that I made in Chapter 15, about Processes.

Break down the steps in what you do and really challenge each step.

Why is it required? Could it be completed in a better way? What would be the impact if it was not completed? Are you doing it for someone external to your team? Do they still need you to do it? Does it need to be completed by your team? Does it align with your Team Purpose, helping you to meet your goals and objectives?

The above are just a few questions to really get you and your team reflecting on what you do and you will be surprised at what it uncovers.

If you decide that something needs to be stopped or changed in how it is completed, the key is to understand whether there are any risks that would be associated with you taking such action.

Do not change things for change's sake, without thinking about any risks that you may expose yourself and your team to.

And remember, if you are reflecting on a process that is regularly going wrong, it is not an opportunity to point fingers but an opportunity to learn and support your colleagues and the team overall in ensuring that changes are made that get rid of the issues that have caused the problem.

FOOD FOR THOUGHT

Q1. How long has it been since you and your team reflected on what you do and discussed whether anything needed to change?

Q2. How often do you and your team have to firefight because something has gone wrong?

Q3. What task takes you the longest time to complete?

Q4. What could you do to reduce the time that it takes?

PING MOMENTS

Time to reflect on this chapter and capture
any ideas that it has given you.

_____

_____

_____

_____

_____

_____

_____

_____

_____

_____

_____

_____

_____

_____

_____

CHAPTER 20:

TRANSFORMATION:
ELEMENT 16 OF 16

*"**Transformation** helps our team create ideas to sow,*
That we agree to implement, to help our team to grow.
For we don't want to stagnate, doing everything the same,
We want to go beyond this, achieving greater fame."

Category: Creative Interactions

Team DyNAmics Definition: The implementation of ideas to change how things are done to become more effective and efficient.

Etymology: From the Latin, meaning to change in shape.

Newbie: Why do we need to change what we do?
Jules: Would you rather our team stood still, or worse, go backwards?

WHAT IS TRANSFORMATION?

"If we do not create ideas that when implemented result in a positive change, as a team we will eventually stagnate, wither and fail."

Transformation is how you adapt what you do because of changes in your working environment. It can be triggered by both external and internal factors that affect your team.

It could be the introduction of new products or services that require you to change the way in which you complete processes. It could be driven by new legislation or governance that has to be complied with. It may be because of new technology that has become available to you, or the removal of old systems.

Changes in resources may also require you to change who undertakes a particular task and how it is completed, and you may also need to transform how things are done, if they repeatedly go wrong.

Whilst Reflection is past orientated and helps you to identify what changes are needed, Transformation is future orientated and helps you to create, agree and implement ideas that support the changes identified.

Transformation should be a constant in your team, as there is always something that can be changed and completed more effectively and efficiently, to get you to an even better place.

I have witnessed teams who have paid scant attention to transforming how they work and invariably cracks begin to appear, and on occasion the team stagnates and begins to fail.

You may have heard of the stages of team development proposed by Bruce Tuckman in 1965. He talked about a team forming, then storming, norming and performing, on their journey to achieving high performance. He later added a fifth stage, which he called adjourning (or mourning), to mark the end of a team's journey.[5]

I believe, however, that by transforming, a team is able to continue on its journey of development and achievement, rather than entering the adjourning phase.

As a former change management specialist, on occasion I would hear people say, "We don't like change."

On trying to understand this further, I found out that what they were actually saying was they did not like change that was imposed upon them.

If you think about it, when we feel we have a personal interest and influence on change, we are OK with it. We change our jobs, where we live, our fashion in clothes, our hairstyles, our relationships with others and I am sure you can think of many other things we change. We find these types of changes OK because we have a personal input and influence on them.

If you think about the recent pandemic and the lockdowns that occurred and all the changes that were imposed upon us, this was a type of change that we had very little or no influence on and hence why a lot of people struggled with coming to terms with what was happening to them.

The key thing when making changes to transform how your team works is ensuring that team members are involved and have an opportunity to shape these changes, by utilising their ideas, skills, knowledge and experience.

BENEFITS

1. It helps to keep the working **Environment** positive.
2. It supports valuing and appreciating **Diversity** within your team.

3. It builds upon the changes that have been highlighted in **Reflection**.
4. It encourages **Collaboration** between team members when implementing solutions.

RED FLAGS

1. Little or no change occurs in the team, with a preference for the status quo.
2. Very few ideas are put forward by team members.
3. When change is mentioned, excuses are voiced, such as "We have too much work to do already".
4. There is an "It will never work" or "What's the point!" attitude to change.

THE STORY
Change of scene

A company that I had been working with for a while asked me to facilitate a session that focussed on increasing the effectiveness of their communication across a department of approximately 150 staff.

They had completed a recent departmental survey and communication had been highlighted as an issue.

There were approximately 12 teams in the department and a "Communication Champion" had volunteered to help transform the communication from each of the teams.

When I met them on the day of the facilitated session in central London, the expectation was that the session would be classroom based. How wrong they were.

I opened the session by reviewing the objectives of the session that they had been made aware of beforehand.

I then opened up with the question, "Where do you get your best ideas?"

One person started by saying their best ideas came when they were out walking their dog.

Another quickly followed with whilst soaking in the bath, and another, walking on the beach.

Walking in the countryside, on the toilet, in bed, after a glass of wine, whilst driving and during the night quickly followed.

I then shared that not one person had said "Whilst sitting at my desk in work".

In fact, in my years of facilitating teamwork, nobody has said this.

It was then that I shared that we would not be in the classroom, we would be out and about.

So, the first thing was to get the group outside of their normal work environment.

The second thing I did was to aid their creativity by given them unusual or different scenarios, as opposed to just saying, "OK, what is wrong with your communication and therefore what needs to be transformed?"

If I had done this, they would more than likely have come up with very few new ideas.

Instead, I put them into three groups of four people each.

To each group I gave a scenario.

Group 1: What if you could only communicate through signs?

Group 2: Which animal or group of animals are excellent at communication?

Group 3: What businesses are good at getting their message across to customers?

I then said that they had three hours to go out into central London, consider the question that I had asked them, apply it to their communication issues and one hour back in the office, to put together a 15-minute presentation to share with their other colleagues and their top three practical ideas that they had come up with for consideration to be implemented.

Even before they left the room, there was a buzz of excitement and energy.

They said that the time just flew by.

Their presentations were inspirational and well thought through and all included three practical ideas, which the other groups thought were great. In fact, during the session, I found out that each group had come up with about ten each.

As each group shared their three top ideas, the individuals in the other groups were allowed to enhance or build upon the ideas shared, by saying, "Yes and we could..."

Finally, the group prioritised the nine ideas that they had come up with, ensuring the ones that would have the biggest impact were implemented first.

Six months later, I found out that they had completed another departmental survey and their scores relating to communication had increased significantly. A short while later I was back at their office and I was able to see and hear for myself how their ideas had been implemented, which was wonderful.

THE SUGGESTION

My suggestions for when you have to transform things in your team are:

1. Involve as many people as possible in your team. Based on behavioural preferences, it will give you a much more holistic view, more varied ideas, different perspectives, the ability to spot any risks and play to people's strengths on implementation.
2. Get out of the office! The most creative outputs from the team development sessions I have facilitated have always been away from the workplace. These have included the top of a mountain in Switzerland, the Saudi Arabian desert, a yacht, a castle, a beach, the Tower of London, The Shard (the tallest building in the UK), Wembley (the home of English Football), the Millennium Stadium (the home of Welsh Rugby), and Gleneagles, one of the most iconic Scottish golf courses.
3. Consider different "what if" scenarios to get people thinking differently.
4. Shortlist ideas generated and prioritise those that will have the biggest positive impact if implemented.
5. Allow individuals to enhance ideas by using "Yes and we could..."
6. Set owners and timescales for implementation.
7. Review the ideas that have been implemented after an agreed period of time, to ensure that they are working as planned. If you are able to measure the benefit of what has been changed, even better, however this will not be possible with everything that you change.

FOOD FOR THOUGHT

Q1. When was the last time that your team discussed ideas to change how your team works?

Q2. How well did the last change that your team implemented go?

Q3. How many people in your team are involved in Transformation? All or a select few?

Q4. What one thing would you change in your team, as you know it would have a positive impact?

PING MOMENTS

Time to reflect on this chapter and capture
any ideas that it has given you.

_____

_____

_____

_____

_____

_____

_____

_____

_____

_____

_____

_____

_____

_____

CHAPTER 21:

EXPLORING LEADERSHIP

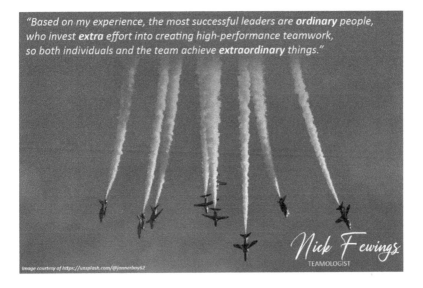

*"Based on my experience, the most successful leaders are **ordinary** people, who invest **extra** effort into creating high-performance teamwork, so both individuals and the team achieve **extraordinary** things."*

Image courtesy of https://unsplash.com/@jannerboy62

As you already know, the main focus of this book has been about teamwork, however I thought it was important, at some point, to explore leadership and share some of the experiences and thoughts that I and others have on this topic. I hope these will help you, whether you are already a leader or are an aspiring team member who no doubt will become a leader at some point in the future.

What I have written in this chapter is obviously not the be-all and end-all of leadership, however it will hopefully provide you with some good advice and a foundation upon which you can explore leadership in more detail, with resources and learning that are dedicated to this subject.

Now a lot of authors put leadership as the top priority of their book, but as you will realise, I have put it after sharing my thoughts and ideas about teamwork.

Why? Because I believe that a leader is another role within a team, albeit one with ultimate responsibility and accountability for the performance of the team.

"Leader, a title used by many, mastered by a few."

Whilst I have had a lot of experience of both leading teams and working with leaders and their teams, I wanted to maximise the benefits for you of reading this book, so in addition to my thoughts about leadership I have also included the thoughts of leaders whom I have had the honour of working with, who have between them many years of leadership experience.

These leaders are all unique, in terms of their leadership style, the industry sectors in which they work and also the size of the organisations and teams that they lead or have led.

They are a mixture of men and women and all of them have one thing in common: they have all been successful in leadership positions and have been valued and appreciated by those that they have led.

These leaders have offered their thoughts about leadership and kindly allowed me to include them in this book. They are in no particular order and appear throughout this chapter.

Having read their thoughts about leadership, I think you will agree that there is a common message and learning that appears in each of their contributions, but rather than telling you what I think it is, I will leave it up to you to make your own decision.

"Over the four decades I have been in business, led and coached teams and leaders of teams, the best leaders have demonstrated authenticity, empathy, purpose, mutuality and known that they cannot know all the answers.

"They know their strengths and weaknesses and ask for help. They go outside their comfort zones to role model how to develop new skills and engage others in their learning.

"They create a safe place to stimulate questioning and dialogue, to be flexible and to manage paradox and complexity.

"They know they are only custodians, and their accountability is to hand over that for which they are responsible in a better shape to the diverse talent they have identified, grown and developed."

— **David May**, Executive Coach and Consultant, Aesara Partners

THERE IS NO MAGIC WAND TO ACHIEVE EXEMPLARY LEADERSHIP

As much as I would like to tell you up front that there is an easy way to achieve high-performance teamwork via your leadership skills, I would be telling you a lie.

Unfortunately, there is no one size fits all when it comes to leading teams effectively. You may have read books that claim otherwise, however speaking from experience and also discussing this with leaders in various organisations, I can categorically say that being a successful leader is dependent on many factors.

There are so many variables. Who you are, what your team does, who is in your team, where your team are located, how many are in your team, whether your team is standalone or is part of a larger process and the impact of changes external to your team environment, to name just a few.

> "Great leadership defines a purpose, a north star, and a supportive culture to engage you on the journey. Done well, leadership inspires you to run faster, aim higher, stretch further in the knowledge that you will be appreciated and encouraged without fear of failure. In fact, great leadership will be ready to catch you when you stumble and is the outstretched hand which helps pull you back up on your feet.

> "Great leadership not only recognises the benefit of diversity of thought, it actively encourages it and embraces differences as a source of value. On a one-to-one basis a great leader builds on an individual's strengths and appreciates their needs. The best leadership enables you to be 'the best me I can be'."

> — **Rowena Innocent**, Group Head of STEM Strategy, Spectris

The analogy that I often make is that leading a team is like playing a game of chess. The pieces are your team members, each with their different behavioural and technical skills, knowledge, ability and experience.

You, as a leader, need to devise and implement strategies to use all the above and create a strategy that enables you and your team to achieve success.

Your opponent is the environment that you and your team work in. On a regular basis, things outside of your control will require you to change your strategy. It may be new legislation, new competitors, changes to products and services or other economic factors.

It could be changes internal to your organisation, a restructure, new products, changes in the top leadership team or a new organisational strategy. I can guarantee one thing, however: the status quo of the environment that you lead your team in will not remain constant for a long period of time.

The key, as a leader, is that you are aware of these changes and adapt your strategy to overcome any challenges and capitalise on opportunities that occur.

So, whilst there is not a universal leadership template to achieve success, I do believe that there are a number of things that you should be doing as a leader that will considerably increase your chances of leading your team to greatness.

"I guess I would describe my leadership as people centric. Surround yourself with talented people who share the same values and give them an opportunity to flourish. This starts at recruitment.

"When looking for new team members, I look for people who are forward thinkers, ambitious and willing to learn, grow and develop. You can teach people skills, but you can't teach attitude and behaviour. Look after your people and understand what is important to them and what motivates them and the results will follow.

"I am a great believer of going for the opportunity – you've got to be in it to win it. We don't always get it right and when that is the case – no problem – fail fast and learn lessons. You will win it the next time!

"And my final influence is probably my Dutch upbringing. Us Dutchies are straight, fair and say it as it is. When I moved to England the best bit of advice I had was to ignore everything that is said before the word 'but' – that's just pleasantries – the real message comes after. I really like your shoes, they are ever so beautiful, but that top you are wearing...

"Feedback is really important to help improve and we need to see this as a gift not an insult. I encourage people to give feedback both positive and constructive – making sure it is timely and based on a real example, explaining what the impact is; and to always reach out for feedback – it is amazing what we can learn – team members, friends and customers in particular can provide valuable insight."

— **Esther McMorris**, Managing Director, Nine Feet Tall

LEADER OR MANAGER?

I think it is important to understand whether you are a leader or a manager.

Both leaders and managers are equally important in business, however what they do is markedly different and it is important to establish which one you are.

In today's business world, the two have become blurred and sometimes that results in those in leadership positions getting confused as to their role and what they need to do.

I do not think this is the fault of the individual, however it is often problematic due to the titles that organisations give to roles. I often see Team Leader being used as a job title, when in fact, based on the job responsibilities and objectives of the role, it clearly should be Team Manager. So, let me provide you with some thoughts that may help clarify things for you.

The word "manager" originally comes from the Latin, manus, meaning hand. So, in my view, managers are hands on, in terms of day-to-day activities that need to be completed, and whilst managing others, more often than not they will not be involved in setting the strategy and vision for their team, which has already been set for them.

"A manager ensures that the team are going in the same direction along a planned route, in a timely fashion. A leader constantly scans the horizon, to decide whether the route needs changing."

Managers focus on the here and now, ensuring tasks are completed efficiently, whereas leaders are looking to the future, creating a compelling and inspirational vision for their team of what they aspire for the team to become and achieve.

The above is merely my take on the difference between a leader and manager and if you search the internet, you will invariably find many other definitions, however you will see a common pattern emerging that should help you better understand whether you are a leader or a manager, irrespective of the title that you have been given by your organisation.

"Effective leadership combines the ability to provide a clear path forward, effective communication about objectives to be achieved and a recognition that without the assistance of those around you, you will almost certainly fail.

"Success as a leader, in my experience, results from facilitating others to do their job well. The qualities that a leader might need to achieve this include generosity, kindness, the ability to listen first as well as clarity of thought and the willingness to lead by example, demonstrably taking responsibility for one's decisions where others might not agree with the decisions that you make, notwithstanding consultation.

"These are not 'soft' qualities. They are qualities that build others, build communities, and build successful businesses. They are the qualities that inspire others, create loyalty and ultimately allow teams to move forward at speed and with conviction."

— **Graham Prisk**, Director, Rame Consulting Limited

THE 80/20 RULE

In one of my leadership roles, my team consisted of approximately 20 people. At this time, the company I worked for had a "Bring Your Son/Daughter to Work Week". It was focussed on young adults who were due to sit their exams and then decide whether they went on to higher education or into work. It was aimed at 15- to 16-year-olds and it provided them with work experience.

Bethany, a daughter of one of my team, joined us for the week, each day sitting with a different member of the team, better understanding what they did in their day-to-day job. The office was open plan, so I could see who she was working with.

At the end of the week, I asked Bethany how she had got on. She let me know that she had thoroughly enjoyed herself and had learnt a lot from those people she had watched doing their jobs.

I then asked her whether she had any questions for me. She had many, however one was particularly interesting, relating to my role as a leader.

Bethany asked me the following question:

"Why are you not at your desk very often? I have watched you and you have spent a lot of your time going around the team and speaking to different people."

My reply was, *"Bethany, that is because I am doing my job, as a leader."*

I explained to her that, as a leader, I had four direct reports, who were managers. They ensured the effectiveness and efficiency of the individuals on their teams in completing day-to-day tasks to meet the objectives that the whole team had been set.

I told her that I spent four of the five days in the week building relationships, inspiring individuals, developing my managers and clarifying our vision for the future, and the other day making changes to strategies and future plans based on the changing working environment, either internally or externally, and evaluating the impact this had on the team that I led.

Bethany, satisfied with my explanation, had another question for me: *"Why do you have four direct reports?"*

I told her that this enabled me to have a detailed 1:1 meeting with each of my managers, once a week, where we discussed short-term progress against their objectives and those of their team, discussed any issues and thoughts on how to overcome them and additionally, spent time on continuing to develop their skillsets and discussed how good our 1:1

relationship was and whether we needed to change anything moving forward.

So, as I had four direct reports, that left one day of our working week for all five of us to get together with the rest of the team, enabling me to share any changes in our vision and future direction, discussing what that meant for day-to-day operations and getting their feedback on how we would implement any changes.

Another thing to consider which may help you work out whether you are a leader or manager is analysing your time. Over a working week, make note of the tasks that you have undertaken, assigning them with how long you spent on them.

At the end of the week, review this list and assign them based on whether the task is operational, ensuring that short-term goals are achieved by you and your team, or whether the task is about the future vision and direction which your team need to move towards and developing the capabilities of your team.

If, when you review the list, significantly less than 80% of your time is spent on future-orientated activities, devising strategies and developing your team, it is likely that your role is more managerial than that of a leader.

However, as I mentioned, both are important roles in an organisation and ultimately, the job title is not important but having clarification about whether you are a leader or a manager is, as it will influence what you do and the amount of time you spend on particular aspects of it.

Even if you decide that your current role is more managerial than leadership, the lessons in this book are still relevant and valuable, as most of them apply to both roles and no doubt, if you are a manager, at some point in the future you will secure a leadership position and therefore need to focus your time and efforts on the future and creating strategies to help your team achieve your short-term goals and longer term vision.

"Exceptional leadership begins with the conception of a clear vision, a clear representation of what aspirational success looks like for your organisation, and requires you to have the ability to articulate your vision in a compelling way at every level of your organisation, and indeed beyond.

"Subsequently, a strategy must be formulated that, if executed flawlessly, would actualise your vision.

"Next, the capabilities required to execute your strategy efficiently and effectively must be identified.

"Further, an organisational structure to house your capabilities in a way that leverages synergy and promotes accountability must be created.

"Procuring the right capabilities into your organisation is key, and the importance of behavioural capabilities, in addition to technical, must not be overlooked or underestimated.

"As a leader, your ongoing imperative is to maintain a cultural paradigm in which everyone believes in the organisation and wants to play their respective part in ensuring its success (either by contributing directly or by helping others to contribute).

"Organisational culture is ephemeral; it must be monitored and adjusted and is contingent on employee values (the hardest and most important attribute to identify).

"Capabilities can be developed; values cannot. Take care to bring people with the right values into your organisation and create an environment in which such people will shine. When you find them, hold on to them: respect them, reward them, retain them. Remember, values create value."

— **Stephen Parker**, Transformative Quality Leader

TECHNICAL EXPERTISE DOES NOT A LEADER MAKE

"As a leader, you will inevitably make mistakes. Success lies within those who treat setbacks as an opportunity to learn from them, so they are not repeated."

"Yes, yes, yes", I thought internally, trying to keep a calm and professional exterior as I left the office of my director and closed the door behind me.

I had set myself a goal of attaining a leadership position by the time I had reached my 30th birthday, and had achieved this goal with a few months to spare. I had been with Barclays for almost ten years, undertaking a variety of technical roles, both working autonomously and also as part of a team.

I was to have a two-week handover of my current job in Exeter before then heading to Poole to complete a two-week handover of my new job. I asked whether there was any personal development planned in terms of leadership. The answer was no, however I was advised that there would be subsequent opportunities.

So, a month later, I handed over the reins of my job to the new incumbent, had a two-week handover of my new role, all whilst trying to sell my family home, buy a new one and sort out the logistics of moving my family to a new area, including school moves for my two young children.

Whilst I was comfortable with the technical aspects of the job, as it was similar to what I had done previously, albeit on a UK-wide scale as opposed to a regional scale, I had never led a team before in my life.

It was not long before I realised that I was out of my depth. Motivating myself to achieve goals and deadlines was a different matter to motivating ten other people on my team.

I asked for confidential and anonymous feedback to help me understand what I was doing wrong and the honest feedback that I received was a lot.

A theme emerged that for a lot of the team, I was not as factual as they wanted, plans were not clear on what we needed to do as a team, and my written communication to them was not as frequent as they would have liked. The way I led myself was obviously not how they needed me to lead them.

It was quite apparent that my lack of leadership training was having a major negative impact on my team.

Now the reason I share this with you is that my story is not an unusual one.

In a survey that I undertook in 2020, via my connections on LinkedIn, over 70% of those who responded, and were in leadership positions, had no formal leadership training prior to taking up their roles!

Even more frightening, of that 70%, 6 out of 10 of them had no formal leadership training after they had taken up their position.

Essentially, in a lot of organisations, those in leadership positions are expected to deliver high performance and achieve goals through their teams, however these organisations are not investing in the development of their leaders to do so.

So, in conclusion, being a technical expert, managing yourself and achieving success does not mean that you can easily step up into a leadership role and achieve similar success leading a team.

My advice would be to insist on leadership development, for the sake of yourself, the sake of your team and ultimately, for the benefit of your organisation.

I say this so you do not need to suffer the trauma, worry and sleepless nights that I did, nor upset and cause problems for those in your team.

"I'm going to use a word which is hardly ever used in books about leadership – or any business books – and that word is love. I think that what it takes to be a great leader is truly to love the people and the business you lead. When you love your business, you are always on the lookout for new opportunities to make it stronger. You cherish your customers. You select your business partners with care. And when you love your team, you want to support them, to train them, to enable them so that they become the best that they can be. You treat them like individuals not a resource. And you forgive them when they make mistakes so that instead of creating a blame culture you create a business where people can own up to their errors, learn from them and grow."

— **Manon Bradley**, Managing Director, Strength2Strength

YOUR ACTIONS SPEAK AS LOUD AS YOUR WORDS

"I love the quote, 'Be yourself, everyone else is already taken' (Oscar Wilde) because for me that's ultimately what leadership is about. Bringing the real you to work. There is no place for ego when you are a leader; you need to be humble, you need to listen and most of all you need to care."

— **Amber Kelly**, Founder, Employees First Ltd

As a leader, you are always in the spotlight, in terms of what you do and how you behave. Your team, your peers, those who may lead you and possibly people in other teams will look at every aspect of what you do and how you behave, to ensure that you practise what you preach, and just because someone cannot hear what you say, do not think for a moment that this will not matter. Let me explain what I mean.

Imagine two of your team. One is close by and one further away. The one nearest to you is able to both hear you and also see your body language and decide whether there is congruence between both.

Now the second team member, who is further away, will not be able to hear what you say, however will still be able to see your body language.

Albert Mehrabian shared a communication model, based on his studies, that suggested that only 7% of communication of feelings and attitudes takes place through the words we use, while 38% takes place through tone and voice and the remaining 55% of communication of these factors takes place through the body language we use.[6]

Now, whilst this model and the percentages attributed have been challenged over the years, what does hold true is that our actions (body language) must align with the words we use and importantly, as human beings, we are able to pick up the context of what another person is saying even if we cannot hear them, via the body language that they exhibit.

So, never forget that there may be team members who are out of earshot, but can still see your body language and again, will be picking up visual clues to try to understand what you are saying. As such, just because someone cannot hear what you are saying, it does not mean that they are not watching you and your leadership style and trying to understand you.

As such, it is important to always be on your best behaviour and demonstrate to your team the behaviour that you expect from them, because if you say one thing to them and demonstrate something different yourself, you will lose their trust in you, which, as we all know, is a difficult thing to rebuild.

"After 28 years at one local authority I found myself suddenly in the position of CEO. The job I admit I had always wanted. Unlike the more usual route of being recruited from somewhere else everyone knew me pretty much, so little opportunity for role playing! But after all, in the words of Gloria Gaynor, 'I am what I am'.

"So for me leadership was, and is, about just being me. Be honest and be authentic. If you're not they'll see through you anyway. I believe to lead you need to inspire, you need to be trusted and you need to live it. Some believe in leading from the front and there are times I've absolutely had to do that but in the main I think I've led from within, being part of the team. Not as easy as it sounds sometimes.

"I believe in leaders encouraging aspiration and allowing people to take chances, and if sometimes things don't go to plan, hold onto your sense of humour. Now that's something I wouldn't get by without.

"Thinking back over recent months and the Covid-19 pandemic I think, more than ever, this approach to leadership is more effective than ever before, and looking forward can stand leaders in good stead as we manage teams in more remote settings and through a myriad of communication channels."

— **Allison Griffin**, former CEO, Sedgemoor District Council

LEADERSHIP ATTRIBUTES

"How you behave towards your staff will influence how they behave towards you."

As a leader, as I've previously mentioned, you are always in the spotlight and therefore it is important that in everything you do and everything you say, you behave in a way that does not upset others due to being inappropriate, as once you have lost the respect and trust of your team, expecting to lead them effectively becomes a tough thing to deliver.

So being on your game, in terms of what you say and how you do things, is vital, as is knowing what attributes people want to see in their leader.

"To me leadership is about being an authentic colleague and friend who is genuine, kind, who takes an interest and who listens. Leadership introduces a whole new environment where everyone is keen to speak

to you and everyone keen to impress you. It is such a humbling and important responsibility to act on that – to take the time to speak to people and more importantly to take the time to listen. They will have successes, challenges, needs and ideas that they want to share. To listen and take action is the most powerful thing a leader can do to show that people are valuable, to show they have a purpose and to show that their perspective matters. Do not waste this very important responsibility – because by looking after your people, by listening and acting, your team will look after you and the business you lead. That to me is what great leadership is all about."

— **David Piltz BSc FIA**, UK Managing Director, Buck

In 2020, I undertook a survey on LinkedIn, simply asking my connections what attributes they wanted to see in their leaders.

The survey received responses from throughout the world, from all sectors and from people in all levels of organisations. Apart from the letter Z, every letter was used by people from Ability right through to Wisdom.

Here are the top four attributes that people responded with, with the definitions from the *Oxford English Dictionary*:

1. Integrity: The quality of being honest and having strong moral principles
2. Passion: An intense desire or enthusiasm for something
3. Visionary: Thinking about or planning the future with imagination or wisdom
4. Empathy: The ability to understand and share the feelings of another

You will notice that none of these words relate to technical abilities; rather, all are behaviours.

As a leader, your team expect to see you demonstrate these attributes and it is therefore important to understand each, know which ones you excel in, those that take you more effort to demonstrate, and importantly, know the appropriate situations when to demonstrate them.

"There's a chief executive I know who has done oodles of media training. You'll have seen her on the TV news and she can often be heard on the Today programme. She once told me she was about to go to do some media training. 'But surely...?' I asked. 'Always take up the offer,' she replied. 'You can always learn something.' And that has stayed with me, as have another leader's wise words that 'Everyone has something to teach and something to learn'.

"But a specific piece of advice? I'd say it applies to anyone leading or managing a team: invest time in getting to know your people.

"My current team is just over two years old and when we started we had a two-day offsite to really get to know each other and work out how to work best together. And since then we've kept it up with regular offsite 'collaborative working days' where we get away from the office together and do a mix of working, problem-solving and socialising. It keeps the creative juices flowing and has helped us deliver effectively as a team.

"In a previous role where I was responsible for leading a team of 80, for the first month I largely did little more than sitting down with all my team members for a lot of coffee. This paid off in spades when managing the group through tight budgets and challenging reorganisations and reprioritisations from the top. It made all the difference in being credible and empathetic with colleagues when having challenging conversations (and the nicer ones too!).

"There are various things you might wish to deprioritise but investing time with your teams should never be one of them."

— **Tim Aldrich**, Assistant Director, Regulatory Reform at the GMC

DON'T LEAD BLIND; GET TOOLED UP

Imagine that one day you were told that you needed to drive a minibus to an agreed destination, with all your team as passengers. Even if you had not driven a minibus before, if you had driven a car I am sure you would feel reasonably confident, wouldn't you?

OK, so you make sure all your team are on board the minibus, have their seatbelts on and you then get into the driver's seat.

To your horror, you look down to where the dashboard and instrument panel are and realise there is nothing there. How confident would you feel now? Probably not that confident. In actual fact, you may even be feeling a bit worried about your ability to complete the journey safely.

Well, that is what leadership in a lot of organisations feels like. Individuals are put into leadership positions and are not provided with either leadership development, nor the tools to enable them to understand their team and how effectively they work together.

Yet organisations expect their leaders to lead their teams to achieve high performance and meet or exceed the targets that their teams are set, as I have already mentioned.

In addition, as part of a straw poll survey of 600 delegates at a conference I spoke at in Singapore, only 25% used personal profiling to understand **WHO** was in their team, and only 1% measured their team effectiveness to understand **HOW** effective their teamwork was.

Both are vital, if you are to achieve high performance in your team, and every leader should use all the appropriate tools that are available to help them and their teams achieve even greater success.

So, if you do not have the tools to understand **WHO** is in your team, nor **HOW** effective your teamwork is, my suggestion would be to seek them out, for your sake and also the sake of your team.

"My thoughts would be that what makes for successful leadership depends on the situation – the people around you, the nature of the challenge; turnaround is different from steady state or growth, PE-backed from listed, small company from large, early stage from mature, tech from industry.

"There are many different types of leader and ways of leading and we are each our own mix of capabilities. Sure, there are some clear things which the books will tell you are important: trustworthiness, competence, an ability to listen (and to hear) and, in this day and age of social media, authenticity (today's politicians have it so wrong!). These are helpful but in truth they are neither necessary nor sufficient.

"The trick is to select, or happen upon, the right leadership situation for you. That requires knowing yourself well and being able to diagnose a leadership situation. The better you are at both these things, the more likely you are to be successful. This is not just because you will select situations better, but also because you will understand what you need to do in any given situation to be successful.

"The more you can then adapt how you approach the leadership situation, the more situations you are likely to succeed in. So my advice to someone starting out? Cut the BS, cut the ego. Go on a journey to understand yourself. Actively hone your ability to diagnose leadership situations.

"Try stuff, make mistakes and continually improve the versatility of your response. And don't fall into one of the most common failure modes I see in leaders – they stop enquiring and adapting and assume that if they just keep applying what has worked for them before, it'll work again."

— **James Thorburn**, CEO, City & County Healthcare Group

THE DYNAMICS OF GREAT TEAMWORK

Understanding our **Team Purpose** is where we must begin,
What this enables and the benefits it will bring.
For this will keep us all on track, give focus to what we do,
Ensuring everything delivered adds positive value.

Trust between each of us we must build deep and strong,
To appreciate each other, so we can get along.
It's vital that we realise that we're stronger as a team,
If we're to work effectively and fulfil our dream.

Plans we need to put in place, so everybody knows,
The steps we all need to take, so we achieve our goals.
Some revisions may be needed, as we all should know,
When changes sometimes happen that are out of our control.

A team is not a team, unless we all **Collaborate**,
Sharing skills and knowledge that we have learnt to date.
For our efforts must be as one, if we are to succeed,
All for one and one for all, a behaviour we must breed.

We each must be **Accountable**, right from the very start,
To deliver quality in our team plan, relating to our part.
Then ensure a smooth handover, to our colleague who is next,
So we can, as a team, create a chain of excellence.

Sometimes things will be easy, sometimes they will be tough,
But if we all go above and beyond, it should hopefully be enough,
By showing our **Commitment**, we surely will pull through,
And demonstrate to others what our team can really do.

Roles and Skills that complement, that is the winning feat,
Like pieces of a jigsaw, they dovetail nice and neat.
Each member of our team, knowing what they and others do,
We all have our part to play, which will help to see us through.

Communication that is effective, so we know what's going on,
Should help us all ensure that nothing does go wrong.
So email, text or face to face, make sure our comms are good,
And whatever is the message, by all it's understood.

Decisions agreed, we must embrace with positivity,
So we move forward as a team, using our ability.
If just one is out of sync, we'll get into a mess,
And sorting out the issue will cause us lots of stress.

Team Meetings, to be effective, must start and end on time,
An agenda sent beforehand, that keeps us all in line.
Actions duly noted, with who does what by when,
Reviewed at our next meeting, before we start again.

Processes are important, to maintain consistency,
Recorded somewhere accessible, so everyone can see.
Then if a process needs to be done by someone totally new,
They have clear instructions of what they need to do.

Everybody feels much better, working in a vibrant place,
As a positive **Environment** will put a smile upon your face,
So whether working remotely, or when we're all together,
Our team should be a great place to work, for all and for forever.

Our **Vision** is the future, what we want to see,
Going from where we are today, to where we want to be.
Stretching yet achievable, so it will inspire,
Individuals and our team, to raise performance higher.

Diversity and respect, so we can celebrate,
Our individuality, and how we operate,
It's just the way we are; there's no right or wrong,
So let's appreciate our differences, so we can get along.

Reflection is important, a chance to stop, look back,
What's gone well in what we've done, and what's taken us off track.
To continue to learn and improve are the things we need,
If we are to perform at our best, and as a team succeed.

Transformation helps our team create ideas to sow,
That we agree to implement, to help our team to grow.
For we don't want to stagnate, doing everything the same,
We want to go beyond this, achieving greater fame.

It is through these 16 Elements, that we'll make our team great,
Our success is down to all of us, in our hands, our fate.
Team DyNAmics helps us achieve what is our dream,
Which we all know is to be a high-performing team.

GET IN TOUCH

I hope that, having read this book, it has provided you with valuable learning about the WHO and the HOW of high-performance teamwork and that it has given you lots of "ping moments" to discuss with your team, helping you to achieve even greater success.

If you feel that it would be beneficial to measure your team effectiveness using the model, so that you have your own Team DyNAmics Report, please do not hesitate to contact me via nick@ngagementworks.com.

ACKNOWLEDGEMENTS

To my wife, Belinda, for her unwavering support, encouragement, ideas and for also giving me a different perspective.

To my mum, for her wise words that "You'll be OK in life, if you can get on with people."

To Mike Jones for opening my eyes to the colourful world of human behaviour.

To Rupert Taylor and Julie Smith (RIP) for their many lessons in exemplary leadership, during my time with Barclays.

To those leaders who provided me with great lessons in how not to lead others. I will not name and shame, but you know who you are.

To those organisations who have either had faith in my ability as a facilitator, to help your teams become more effective, or as a conference speaker, to share my experience, to help delegates achieve high-performance teamwork.

To Clarity4D, for producing the highly-regarded personal development profiles that I have successfully used with many individuals and teams. Also for partnering with me, so that the Team DyNAmics Model can be used by teams around the world, to enhance their team effectiveness.

And in no particular order, to Graham Prisk, Stephen Parker, Manon Bradley, Esther McMorris, Allison Griffin, Tim Aldrich, James Thorburn, David May, David Piltz, Amber Kelly and Rowena Innocent, who I have had the opportunity and joy of knowing and who, in my opinion, have demonstrated their own unique and successful style of leadership, and have kindly submitted a paragraph on what exemplary leadership means to them.

To Karen Williams, The Book Mentor and creator of The Smart Author System, without whom this book would still be in my head.

To Samantha Pearce, SWATT Books, for the design and style of this book, to complement the learning within it.

To Louise Lubke Cuss, Wordblink, for her editing and proofreading, which was invaluable in correcting my many grammatical errors.

To Andrea Sexton, Admire PR, for helping to get the message out there about this book.

And last but not least, to family, friends and business contacts, who provided me with feedback, ideas, suggestions and the motivation to keep going.

Thank you all, as without you, nobody would be reading this.

ABOUT THE AUTHOR

Nick Fewings, Teamologist, initially had a 20-year career with Barclays, working his way up from a clerk in branch banking, to a change leader, leading the people workstreams of global projects.

For the past 20 years, Nick has specialised in learning and development, facilitating team development around the globe and, in doing so, helping teams to achieve high performance.

He has profiled thousands of individuals and worked with hundreds of teams.

Nick is the creator of the Team DyNAmics Model that measures team effectiveness across 16 areas of teamwork, helping teams to achieve high-performance teamwork.

When not facilitating, Nick is a highly-regarded conference speaker, having spoken at over 500 conferences worldwide about how to achieve high-performance teamwork.

Nick was born in Plymouth, in the county of Devon in the UK, a city famous as the place where the Pilgrim Fathers set sail to colonise America in 1620.

An only son to a nurse and dockyard worker, he went to Devonport High School for Boys before joining Barclays Bank.

Since childhood, he has passionately supported the city's football team Plymouth Argyle.

Nick currently lives on the south coast of the UK, in Dorset, with his wife and their Greek rescue dog, Lucy.

Nick has many interests, including walks by the coast or in the countryside. Being a people person and family man, he loves nothing better than meeting up with family and friends, and spending time with his grandchildren.

Nick's other interests include photography, travel and live music but definitely not DIY.

ENDNOTES

1   Half of UK workers quit due to bad management – Personnel Today article, 3rd September 2019, https://www.personneltoday.com/hr/half-of-uk-managers-quit-due-to-bad-management/

2   Interview with Pilar Zeta, 20th December 2015, https://www.coldplay.com/interview-pilar-zeta-ahfod-artwork-creator/

3   UK workers waste a year of their lives in useless meetings – Management Today article, https://www.managementtoday.co.uk/uk-workers-waste-year-lives-useless-meetings/article/1175002

4   Diversity definition, https://www.ferris.edu/administration/president/DiversityOffice/Definitions.htm

5   Bruce Tuckman's stages of team development, https://en.wikipedia.org/wiki/Bruce_Tuckman

6   Albert Mehrabian, https://www.bl.uk/people/albert-mehrabian

NICK FEWINGS

CPSIA information can be obtained
at www.ICGtesting.com
Printed in the USA
LVHW070606010322
712229LV00012B/376